CHRISTIANITY AND ECONOMICS
IN THE POST–COLD WAR ERA

Christianity and Economics in the Post–Cold War Era

The Oxford Declaration and Beyond

Edited by

Herbert Schlossberg,
Vinay Samuel, and
Ronald J. Sider

WILLIAM B. EERDMANS PUBLISHING COMPANY
GRAND RAPIDS, MICHIGAN

Copyright © 1994 by Wm. B. Eerdmans Publishing Co.
255 Jefferson Ave. S.E., Grand Rapids, Michigan 49503

Printed in the United States of America

00 99 98 97 96 95 94   7 6 5 4 3 2 1

ISBN 0-8028-0798-4

Contents

CONTENTS

PART III

PART IV

Preface

The Oxford Conference on Christian Faith and Economics is an ongoing cooperative effort. It seeks to discover and promulgate ways in which people can order their economic affairs in accordance with the insights and mandates of biblical teaching. Its basic assumption is that the economic aspect of life, like all other aspects of life, must be brought under submission to God's will and that once it is it enjoys the blessings that the Bible says are in store for those who are obedient to the divine commands. From the start, in the midst of serious disagreements about what all this means, the participants in the conference have been united in the conviction that the Lordship of Christ is central to this enterprise and that its success is dependent on God's blessing and on conformity with God's will.

Ronald Sider explains in the opening chapter of this book how the conference began and traces its course through the conclusion of its second major meeting, which was held in January 1990. "The Oxford Declaration on Christian Faith and Economics" has been the major written result of the ongoing Oxford Conference and is the focus of this book. The text of the Declaration follows Dr. Sider's Introduction.

There follow in Part II six chapters dealing with various facets of economic life: Miroslav Volf discusses the theological implications of work and the role of the Holy Spirit. Joe Remenyi and Bill Taylor address the fostering of entrepreneurial efforts among poor people through the provision of credit. Calvin Beisner and Stephen Mott follow with chapters that stem from the debates in Oxford over the meaning of justice in biblical perspective. P. J. Hill examines the implications of government power on economic life. And finally Herbert Schlossberg discusses the role of capital formation, which he believes was slighted in the Declaration.

Part III contains four chapters stemming from the appearance at roughly the same time as the Oxford Declaration of parallel efforts with regard to the relation between Christian faith and economic life from other parts of the church spectrum — from the World Council of Churches and the Roman Catholic Church. Michael Novak and Derek Cross compare the Declaration with the papal encyclical *Centesimus Annus*. Donald Hay adds to those two documents a third from the World Council, "Economy as a Matter of Faith." Lawrence Adams and Fredrick Jones consider the Oxford Declaration in comparison with another World Council document, this one centering on what the Council believes is an environmental crisis. Rob van Drimmelen rounds out this section with a comparison of the Declaration and a third World Council study document.

Finally, James Skillen provides a general critique of the Oxford Declaration and suggests avenues for future work.

The Oxford Conference is an ongoing process. In February 1995 Oxford III will convene in New Delhi, India, to assess the impact of the market economy on the Third World and the former Soviet Union.

PART I

Introduction

Ronald J. Sider

It has not been a common experience to hear liberation-oriented theologians affirming free-market strategies or conservative market economists demanding a special focus on justice for the poor. But that is exactly what happened at the ground-breaking Conference on Christian Faith and Economics held at Oxford, January 4-9, 1990. Vigorous critics of democratic capitalism endorsed democracy, while its staunch defenders condemned the way centralized economic power, consumerism, racism, and dehumanization of workers often plague capitalist societies.

The conference gathered together an enormously diverse group of over one hundred evangelical leaders from all the continents and from very different ideological backgrounds — bankers, theologians, economists, ethicists, business leaders, and development practitioners.

Participants included top economists like Dr. Raja Chelliah, a member and former head of the Indian Planning Commission (India's council of economic advisers) for the previous five years; prominent evangelical Latin American theologians like Dr. Rene Padilla who have learned from liberation theology; community development leaders like Evelyn Feliciano and Ruth Callanta from the Philippines; and Arthur Block, a leading Canadian businessman. A major group of articulate American conservative leaders was also there, including economist P. J. Hill of Wheaton College, Tom Rose from Grove City College, Herb Schlossberg from the Fieldstead Institute, Doug Bandow from the libertarian Cato Institute, Ken Myers from the Villars Committee on Relief and Development, and Michael Cromartie from the Ethics and Public Policy Center.

In some opening remarks I confessed that I was not ready to bet my pension that such a diverse group of people could say anything significant together. But we did. For two reasons. First, we truly listened to people from other situations. American conservatives heard the cry of Latin Americans overwhelmed with crushing debt payments. And the Latin Americans in turn heard conservative North Americans' arguments for a market economy. Second, and even more importantly, as evangelicals we were committed to submit to the authority of the Scriptures.

I still have a vivid memory of my strong pessimism about the outcome of the conference as I flew across the blustery North Atlantic in early January 1990. As General Secretary of the Steering Committee, I had been hard at work on the process for several years. During the flight to London, I had to assign people to small groups so that each group would reflect the range of views, continents, races, and genders at the conference. As I reflected on the vast range of people assembling, I wondered to myself whether it would be possible for this incredibly diverse group to agree on anything significant that they could affirm together! I was doubtful. I thought perhaps the conference would be a long, useless argument.

Conservative author and economist, E. Calvin Beisner, apparently also had low expectations as he traveled. He feared conservatives would not get a fair hearing.

But something important happened at Oxford. We listened to each other! We also worshiped and prayed together. A strong commitment to Jesus Christ helped bridge our many differences. So did our commitment to the authority of Scripture and our desire for careful factual analysis. All were determined to submit to the full authority of Scripture. All wanted to follow wherever biblical truth and factual analysis might lead.

At the end, Cal Beisner praised the "organizers' firm commitment to open discussion, biblical authority, and fidelity to empirical economic facts."[1] Professor Richard Chewning of Baylor University's School of Business confided to the whole conference near the end that never in his thirty-two years of professional life had he been at a conference so diverse, so open, and so unified at the same time. As we prayed, worshiped, and studied the Scriptures and economic reality together, bridges were built across some very deep divides.

The process began several years earlier in a conversation between

1. *Christianity Today,* March 19, 1990, p. 52.

Vinay Samuel and myself. Chris Sugden and David Bussau soon joined in the planning.[2] We were all engaged in different ways in trying to empower the poor. Through the international journal *Transformation,* Vinay, Chris, and I were also working together promoting evangelical dialogue on social ethics across all the lines that divide us. Taking on the "big" debate over economics seemed like a large but not impossible task.

So we made plans to call together a small but very diverse group of evangelical leaders from around the world to set an agenda for integrating careful biblical analysis and careful economic analysis in the hope that the result might be a more biblically informed understanding of economics.

The letter of invitation sent out by Vinay, David, and myself spelled out our hopes:

> Christians have been struggling with economic issues from the very beginning of the church. But evangelical Christians have not brought adequate biblical expertise and economic sophistication to the task of developing a profoundly biblical perspective to economic life. Such a task, of course, will take years — indeed it will never be completed. This consultation is designed to set the agenda.
>
> Specifically:
>
> 1) We want to clarify the main areas of conflict between the basic economic systems operating in the world today.
>
> 2) We want to clarify the biblical resources relevant to current economic issues.
>
> 3) We want to specify and develop Christian alternatives to current economic systems and activities.
>
> 4) We want to plan a several-year process that will facilitate these objectives.

We decided not merely to assemble friends and colleagues who shared our basic assumptions and analysis. We wanted genuine listening across a number of barriers that are seldom crossed.[3] So we invited

---

2. Throughout the Oxford Conference process, David Bussau has played a quiet but vital role in managing and (with Vinay Samuel) raising the necessary funds.

3. For a statement of my concern to build such bridges, see my article published at the time: "A Plea for More Radical Conservatives and More Conserving Radicals," *Transformation,* January-March 1987, pp. 11-16 (especially the covenant on p. 15).

bankers, business leaders, economists, theologians, ethicists, and biblical scholars. We invited socioeconomic conservatives and liberals. And we invited people from all continents.

Thirty-six leaders assembled at Oxford University in January 1987 for the first Oxford Conference on Christian Faith and Economics. From the inaugural address by Sir Fred Catherwood (a member of the European Parliament) through vigorous debate over papers and responses by people like Nicholas Wolterstorff, Samuel Escobar, Herb Schlossberg, Stephen Mott, Milton Wan, P. J. Hill, Washington Okumu, and Bob Goudzwaard, the conference proved to be useful. In fact, by the end we felt so certain that the dialogue among such diverse people was important that we decided to extend and deepen the debate. A final conference report outlined areas of agreement and disagreement. It also called for an expanded Steering Committee to develop two studies in the intervening three years: (1) a "comprehensive Christian perspective on the economy" and (2) an analysis of micro income generation projects among the poor.[4]

The first conference had been organized essentially by Vinay Samuel, David Bussau, Chris Sugden, and myself. In January 1987, we expanded the Steering Committee so that it more closely reflected the diversity of views, continents, and professions represented at Oxford.[5]

Three years of preparation for Oxford II followed. Rothangliani Rema Chhangte, a gifted Indian graduate student at Eastern College and Eastern Baptist Theological Seminary, helped me organize the international regional process. In six regions of the world, people gathered in regional conferences to discuss papers prepared in their particular regions on four topics: stewardship and creation, work and leisure, justice, and freedom, government, and economics.

Dr. Roy McCloughry, a British economist, working with Dr. Miroslav Volf, a Yugoslav theologian, examined all the regional material

---

4. For the full report and list of the participants, see *Transformation*, April-June 1987, pp. 22-24. A combined issue of *Transformation* (July-September and October-December 1987) contains all the papers presented at Oxford I.

5. The following persons served on the Steering Committee: Vinay Samuel (India) as Chairman, Ronald J. Sider (USA) as General Secretary, David Bussau (Australia) as Treasurer, Arthur Block (Canada), John K. Chang (Philippines), Samuel Escobar (USA/Peru), Bob Goudzwaard (Netherlands), P. J. Hill (USA), Gerrishon K. Ikiara (Kenya), Friedrich Manske (Germany), Rob Martin (USA), Bryant Myers (USA), Chris Sugden (UK), Herbert Schlossberg (USA), and K. William Taylor (Australia).

plus the papers from Oxford I and prepared a large summary document. They also produced a draft declaration on Christian faith and economics.

At the same time, a team led by William Taylor (an Australian businessman) and Dr. Joe Remenyi (an Australian professor of economics) conducted a large empirical study of representative income generation programs in Asia, Africa, and Latin America. Their report, along with the work of Hernando de Soto, was to play a significant role at Oxford II.

As we worked on the list of invitees for 1990, we sought to bring together the full range of viewpoints in the evangelical community. A careful look at the list of participants demonstrates that we succeeded to a striking degree. In fact, the participants were so diverse that I doubted, as I noted earlier, whether we could go beyond platitudes.[6]

I believe that we did — though others will have to judge where we managed genuine breakthroughs in understanding and where we merely papered over disagreement. Some of both occurred.

To the extent that we achieved significant new agreements, I believe it was because of several factors. Everyone shared a deep desire to submit all their thinking to the authority of the Scriptures. We also took time for common worship and Bible study. Strong, too, was a shared desire to get our "economic facts straight."

Some have suggested that the collapse of communism played a significant role. I think that had some significance, but I suspect its importance has been overstated.

The report on micro income generation projects by Taylor and Remenyi was undoubtedly important.[7] Everyone — both those who tended to be critical of elements of the market economy and those who had been its defenders — agreed enthusiastically that promoting small businesses through micro loans to poor entrepreneurs was one of the very hopeful ways to implement the biblical call to justice for the poor.[8]

---

6. The vast majority of the participants at Oxford II signed the final document. See *Transformation,* April-June 1990, p. 9, for the list.

7. William Taylor chaired the committee that did the study on income generation. For the final study, see Joe Remenyi, *Where Credit Is Due: Income Generating Programmes for the Poor in Developing Countries* (London: Intermediate Technology Publications, 1991).

8. For the official conference "Statement on Income Generation Programmes among the Poor in Developing Countries," see *Transformation,* April-June 1990, pp. 10-11.

The debates flowed fast and furious. Participants got ideological speeches off their chests. But we also listened to each other. Sharing personal pilgrimages helped bring us together. Raja J. Chelliah traced his pilgrimage from his early hope that socialism would solve India's problems to his current conviction that a market economy would better serve the goal of justice.[9]

As secretary of the Drafting Committee I can report from vivid experience that we had a tough task. The diverse viewpoints at the conference were well represented in our committee.[10] The chairman, Rene Padilla, struggled successfully to hold us together and bring us to agreement. Hot arguments eventually resulted in carefully crafted phrases that received further debate in intense plenary sessions.

Padilla's wise oversight of the drafting process contributed greatly to our success. At the beginning of our work on the text, he reminded everyone that the first thing one does when one looks at a group photo is to find oneself. He suggested that the final document should bear some resemblance to a group photo in that everyone should be represented. But that would not mean a weak document filled only with general platitudes. Rather it would mean a strong document that honestly reflected both agreements and disagreements.

Intense disagreements did, in fact, abound. Scores of frequently contradictory submissions flowed into the drafting committee. Padilla often assigned two people representing the two sides of the debate to go aside and thrash out a sentence or a paragraph that both could accept with integrity. Sometimes they discovered a surprising degree of consensus. Sometimes they could only carefully and fairly state their differences. When people complained that the process was too slow, Padilla replied, "No, we must listen to everyone."

In a recent conversation, Rene shared this evaluation of his leadership of the Drafting Committee: "If I made any contribution to the drafting process, it was to make sure that everyone had a chance to be

9. "Economics and Christian Faith: A Personal Pilgrimage," *Transformation*, April-June 1990, pp. 15-17.

10. The following persons served on the Drafting Committee: Pedro Arana (Peru), Ruth Callanta (Philippines), P. J. Hill (USA), Gerrishon K. Ikiara (Kenya), Roy McCloughry (UK), Stephen Mott (USA), Bryant Myers (USA), Kenneth A. Myers (USA), Rene Padilla (Argentina), Ronald J. Sider (USA), Bill Taylor (Australia), and Miroslav Volf (Germany/Yugoslavia).

heard and represented in what the document said. I did that because I am committed to a democratic process, whether in the life of the church or in society."[11]

When our work was finally finished, we felt a general sense of exhilaration. I still vividly recall my own sense of astonished delight. Tom Rose of Grove City College concluded: "It is evident to me that the Holy Spirit has worked in a positive and wonderful way among us."[12] Kim Hawtrey, chief economist for the State Bank of Sydney, Australia, added: "The gaping distances between our continents, our schools of thought and between apparently opposite ideas — distances which previously seemed insurmountable — became the very location for new bridges linking us together."[13] Thailand's Dr. Kriengsak Chareonwongsak (an economist and international leader in the charismatic movement) said: "The richness that emerged from these discussions was invaluable and could never have been achieved through individual study. I deeply appreciated the common desire to find the truth anchored in the Word of God."[14]

Professor Hermann Sautter (University of Frankfurt) put it this way:

> I never before saw so many Christians from so many different backgrounds discussing economic issues seriously. They all carried their national perspectives with them: Australians were opposed to accepting any strong statement against the exploitation of natural resources. North Americans were inclined to stress the free market-system. Latin Americans were particularly interested in putting their international debt problem on the agenda.
>
> All seemed to have good economic reasons for their arguments, but discussing them opened our eyes to many underlying value-judgements. This was possible because there was one common perspective — the biblical one. It was more important than any other point of view, and in the light of Christian faith national and cultural values were put in their proper place. Economics could be understood as economics, not as a kind of secular doctrine of salvation. We learned

---

11. Personal conversation with Rene Padilla, February 15, 1993.
12. *Transformation,* April-June 1990, p. 6.
13. Ibid., p. 1.
14. *Transformation,* July-September 1990, p. 32.

much from each other. Overall we learned that we form an international community of Christians, and that the truth of Christian faith may be discovered in its full extent only in sharing this community.[15]

Subsequent responses to the Oxford Declaration confirmed our immediate sense of elation. News reports and critical analyses followed quickly.[16] A person closely connected to the World Council of Churches' 1992 declaration on "Christian Faith and the World Economy" reported to Vinay Samuel that the Oxford Declaration was a major influence in the preparation of that ecumenical document.

The following chapters of this volume represent an attempt to assess the significance of the Oxford Declaration. Only subsequent history, of course, will determine its long-term importance. But for those of us who were present, it was a high point of vigorous debate and mutual learning, never to be forgotten.[17]

15. *Transformation,* April-June 1990, p. 5.

16. News stories and responses have included "Stewardship in the 90s: Two Views," *Economic Studies Program Briefing Paper,* July 1990, no. 1 (Washington, D.C.: The Institute on Religion and Democracy); Lawrence Adams and Fredrick Jones, "Christianity and Economics: New Documents for the 90s," *Religion & Economics Quarterly,* Summer 1990; Doug Bandow, "Evangelical Perestroika in Oxford," *The Wall Street Journal,* April 24, 1990; E. Calvin Beisner, "Opposites Come Together at Oxford," *World,* January 27, 1990, pp. 8-9; "Ideology Succumbs to Unity in Oxford," *Christianity Today,* March 19, 1990, p. 52; Wally Kroeker, "A Declaration from Oxford on Faith and Economics," *The Marketplace,* March/April 1990, pp. 16-18; Ronald J. Sider, "A Trickle-Up Response to Poverty," *ESA Advocate,* March 1990; *idem,* "Let's Be Fair," *World,* March 24, 1990, p. 22; James W. Skillen, "Christian Faith and Economics: An Important New Declaration," *Public Justice Report* 13, no. 6, March 1990, p. 1; Loren Wilkinson, "Christian Economists Side with Free Markets," *Christian Week,* February 6, 1990, p. 5; see also *Stewardship Journal* 1, no. 1 (Winter 1991), which has three responses to the Oxford Declaration.

17. I want to acknowledge the important assistance of Rothangliani Chhangte in preparing this chapter.

The Oxford Declaration on Christian Faith and Economics*

Preamble

This **Oxford Declaration on Christian Faith and Economics** of January 1990 is issued jointly by over one hundred theologians and economists, ethicists and development practitioners, church leaders and business managers who come from various parts of the world. We live in diverse cultures and subcultures, are steeped in differing traditions of theological and economic thinking, and therefore have diverse notions as to how Christian faith and economic realities should intersect.[1] We have found this diversity enriching even when we could not reach agreement. At the same time we rejoice over the extent of unanimity on the complex economics of today made possible by our common profession of faith in our Lord Jesus Christ.

We affirm that through his life, death, resurrection, and ascension to glory, Christ has made us one people (Galatians 3:28). Though living in different cultures, we acknowledge together that there is one body

---

*The Oxford Declaration was first published in *Transformation,* April/June 1990, pp. 1-8.

1. In January 1987, 36 Christians from all continents and a broad range of professions and socio-political perspectives came together at Oxford to discuss contemporary economic issues in a way that was both faithful to the scriptures and grounded in careful economic analysis. (The papers from that conference were published in *Transformation* 4 [1987], nr. 3.4.) They authorized a three year process to attempt to draft a comprehensive statement on Christian faith and economics. In this project, groups of economists and theologians met all over the world in regional conferences and addressed issues under four headings: Stewardship and Creation; Work and Leisure; The Definition of Justice and Freedom; Government and Economics. A separate paper on micro enterprise was also undertaken. These regional discussions and studies were then drawn together to form the issues for analysis and debate at the Second Oxford Conference on January 4-9, 1990.

and one Spirit, just as we are called to the one hope, one Lord, one faith, one baptism, and one God and Father of us all (Ephesians 4:4).

We acknowledge that a Christian search for truth is both a communal and also an individual effort. As part of the one people in Christ, each of us wants to comprehend the relevance of Christ to the great issues facing humanity today together "with all the saints" (Ephesians 3:18). All our individual insights need to be corrected by the perspectives of the global Christian community as well as Christians through the centuries.

We affirm that Scripture, the word of the living and true God, is our supreme authority in all matters of faith and conduct. Hence we turn to Scripture as our reliable guide in reflection on issues concerning economic, social, and political life. As economists and theologians we desire to submit both theory and practice to the bar of Scripture.

Together we profess that God, the sovereign of life, in love made a perfect world for human beings created to live in fellowship with God. Although our greatest duty is to honour and glorify God, we rebelled against God, fell from our previous harmonious relationship with God, and brought evil upon ourselves and God's world. But God did not give up on the creation. As Creator, God continues patiently working to overcome the evil which was perverting the creation. The central act of God's redemptive new creation is the death, resurrection, and reign in glory of Jesus Christ, the Son of God, and the sending of the Holy Spirit. This restoration will only be completed at the end of human history and the reconciliation of all things. Justice is basic to Christian perspectives on economic life.

Justice is rooted in the character of God. "For the Lord is righteous, he loves justice" (Psalm 11:7). Justice expresses God's actions to restore God's provision to those who have been deprived and to punish those who have violated God's standards.

A. Creation and Stewardship

God the Creator

1. From God and through God and to God are all things (Romans 11:36). In the freedom of God's eternal love, by the word of God's omnipotent power, and through the Creator Spirit, the Triune God gave being to

the world and to human beings which live in it. God pronounced the whole creation good. For its continuing existence creation is dependent on God. The same God who created it is present in it, sustaining it, and giving it bountiful life (Psalm 104:29). In Christ, "all things were created . . . and all things hold together" (Colossians 1:15-20). Though creation owes its being to God, it is itself not divine. The greatness of creation — both human and non-human — exists to glorify its Creator. The divine origin of the creation, its continued existence through God, redemption through Christ, and its purpose to glorify God are fundamental truths which must guide all Christian reflection on creation and stewardship.

Stewardship of Creation

2. God the Creator and Redeemer is the ultimate owner. "The earth is the Lord's and the fullness thereof" (Psalm 24:1). But God has entrusted the earth to human beings to be responsible for it on God's behalf. They should work as God's stewards in the creative, faithful management of the world, recognising that they are responsible to God for all they do with the world and to the world.

3. God created the world and pronounced it "very good" (Genesis 1:31). Because of the Fall and the resulting curse, creation "groans in travail" (Romans 8:22). The thoughtlessness, greed, and violence of sinful human beings have damaged God's good creation and produced a variety of ecological problems and conflicts. When we abuse and pollute creation, as we are doing in many instances, we are poor stewards and invite disaster in both local and global eco-systems.

4. Much of human aggression toward creation stems from a false understanding of the nature of creation and the human role in it. Humanity has constantly been confronted by the two challenges of selfish individualism, which neglects human community, and rigid collectivism, which stifles human freedom. Christians and others have often pointed out both dangers. But only recently have we realised that both ideologies have a view of the world with humanity at the centre which reduces material creation to a mere instrument.

5. Biblical life and world view is not centred on humanity. It is God-centred. Non-human creation was not made exclusively for human beings. We are repeatedly told in the Scripture that all things — human

13

beings and the environment in which they live — were "for God" (Romans 11:36; 1 Corinthians 8:6; Colossians 1:16). Correspondingly, nature is not merely the raw material for human activity. Though only human beings have been made in the image of God, non-human creation too has a dignity of its own, so much so that after the flood God established a covenant not only with Noah and his descendants, but also "with every living creature that is with you" (Genesis 9:9). Similarly, the Christian hope for the future also includes creation. "The creation itself will be set free from its bondage to decay and obtain the glorious liberty of the children of God" (Romans 8:21).

6. The dominion which God gave human beings over creation (Genesis 1:30) does not give them licence to abuse creation. First, they are responsible to God, in whose image they were made, not to ravish creation but to sustain it, as God sustains it in divine providential care. Second, since human beings are created in the image of God for community and not simply as isolated individuals (Genesis 1:28), they are to exercise dominion in a way that is responsible to the needs of the total human family, including future generations.

7. Human beings are both part of creation and also unique. Only human beings are created in the image of God. God thus grants human beings dominion over the non-human creation (Genesis 1:28-30). But dominion is not domination. According to Genesis 2:15, human dominion over creation consists in the twofold task of "tilling and taking care" of the garden. Therefore all work must have not only a productive but also a protective aspect. Economic systems must be shaped so that a healthy ecological system is maintained over time. All responsible human work done by the stewards of God the Sustainer must contain an element of cooperation with the environment.

Stewardship and Economic Production

8. Economic production results from the stewardship of the earth which God assigned to humanity. While materialism, injustice, and greed are in fundamental conflict with the teaching of the whole Scripture, there is nothing in Christian faith that suggests that the production of new goods and services is undesirable. Indeed, we are explicitly told that God "richly furnishes us with everything to enjoy" (1 Timothy 6:17). Production is not only necessary to sustain life and make it enjoyable;

it also provides an opportunity for human beings to express their creativity in the service of others. In assessing economic systems from a Christian perspective, we must consider their ability both to generate and to distribute wealth and income justly.

Technology and its Limitations

9. Technology mirrors the basic paradox of the sinfulness and goodness of human nature. Many current ecological problems result from the extensive use of technology after the onset of industrialization. Though technology has liberated human beings from some debasing forms of work, it has also often dehumanised other forms of work. Powerful nations and corporations that control modern technology are regularly tempted to use it to dominate the weak for their own narrow self-interest. As we vigorously criticise the negative effects of technology, we should, however, not forget its positive effects. Human creativity is expressed in the designing of tools for celebration and work. Technology helps us meet the basic needs of the world population and to do so in ways which develop the creative potential of individuals and societies. Technology can also help us reverse environmental devastation. A radical rejection of modern technology is unrealistic. Instead we must search for ways to use appropriate technology responsibly according to every cultural context.

10. What is technologically possible is not necessarily morally permissible. We must not allow technological development to follow its own inner logic, but must direct it to serve moral ends. We acknowledge our limits in foreseeing the impact of technological change and encourage an attitude of humility with respect to technological innovation. Therefore continuing evaluation of the impact of technological change is essential. Four criteria derived from Christian faith help us to evaluate the development and use of technology. First, technology should not foster disintegration of family or community, or function as an instrument of social domination. Second, persons created in the image of God must not become mere accessories of machines. Third, as God's stewards, we must not allow technology to abuse creation. If human work is to be done in cooperation with creation then the instruments of work must cooperate with it too. Finally, we should not allow technological advancements to become objects of false worship or

seduce us away from dependence on God (Genesis 11:1-9). We may differ in what weight we ascribe to individual criteria in concrete situations and therefore our assessment of particular technologies may differ. But we believe that these criteria need to be taken into consideration as we reflect theologically on technological progress.

11. We urge individuals, private institutions, and governments everywhere to consider both the local, immediate, and the global, long term ecological consequences of their actions. We encourage corporate action to make products which are more "environmentally friendly." And we call on governments to create and enforce just frameworks of incentives and penalties which will encourage both individuals and corporations to adopt ecologically sound practices.

12. We need greater international cooperation between individuals, private organisations, and nations to promote environmentally responsible action. Since political action usually serves the self-interest of the powerful, it will be especially important to guarantee that international environmental agreements are particularly concerned to protect the needs of the poor. We call on Christians everywhere to place high priority on restoring and maintaining the integrity of creation.

B. Work and Leisure

Work and Human Nature

13. Work involves all those activities done, not for their own sake, but to satisfy human needs. Work belongs to the very purpose for which God originally made human beings. In Genesis 1:26-28, we read that God created human beings in his image "in order to have dominion over . . . all the earth." Similarly, Genesis 2:15 tells us that God created Adam and placed him in the garden of Eden to work in it, to "till it and keep it." As human beings fulfil this mandate, they glorify God. Though fallen, as human beings "go forth to their work" (Psalm 104:23) they fulfil an original purpose of the Creator for human existence.

14. Because work is central to the Creator's intention for humanity, work has intrinsic value. Thus work is not solely a means to an end. It is not simply a chore to be endured for the sake of satisfying human desires or needs, especially the consumption of goods. At the same time, we have to guard against over-valuation of work. The essence of human

beings consists in that they are made in the image of God. Their ultimate, but not exclusive, source of meaning and identity does not lie in work, but in becoming children of God by one Spirit through faith in Jesus Christ.

15. For Christians, work acquires a new dimension. God calls all Christians to employ through work the various gifts that God has given them. God calls people to enter the kingdom of God and to live a life in accordance with its demands. When people respond to the call of God, God enables them to bear the fruit of the Spirit and endows them individually with multiple gifts of the Spirit. As those who are gifted by the Spirit and whose actions are guided by the demands of love, Christians should do their work in the service of God and humanity.

The Purpose of Work

16. In the Bible and in the first centuries of the Christian tradition, meeting one's needs and the needs of one's community (especially its underprivileged members) was an essential purpose of work (Psalm 128:2; 2 Thessalonians 3:8; 1 Thessalonians 4:9-12; Ephesians 4:28; Acts 20:33-35). The first thing at issue in all fields of human work is the need of human beings to earn their daily bread and a little more.

17. The deepest meaning of human work is that the almighty God established human work as a means to accomplish God's work in the world. Human beings remain dependent on God, for "unless the Lord builds the house, those who build it labour in vain" (Psalm 127:1a). As Genesis 2:5 suggests, God and human beings are co-labourers in the task of preserving creation.

18. Human work has consequences that go beyond the preservation of creation to the anticipation of the eschatological transformation of the world. They are, of course, not ushering in the kingdom of God, building the "new heavens and a new earth." Only God can do that. Yet their work makes a small and imperfect contribution to it — for example, by shaping the personalities of the citizens of the eternal kingdom which will come through God's action alone.

19. However, work is not only a means through which the glory of human beings as God's stewards shines forth. It is also a place where the misery of human beings as impeders of God's purpose becomes visible. Like the test of fire, God's judgment will bring to light the work

which has ultimate significance because it was done in cooperation with God. But it will also manifest the ultimate insignificance of work done in cooperation with those evil powers which scheme to ruin God's good creation (1 Corinthians 3:12-15).

Alienation in Work

20. Sin makes work an ambiguous reality. It is both a noble expression of human creation in the image of God, and, because of the curse, a painful testimony to human estrangement from God. Whether human beings are tilling the soil in agrarian societies, or operating high-tech machinery in information societies, they work under the shadow of death, and experience struggle and frustration in work (Genesis 3:17-19).

21. Human beings are created by God as persons endowed with gifts which God calls them to exercise freely. As a fundamental dimension of human existence, work is a personal activity. People should never be treated in their work as mere means. We must resist the tendency to treat workers merely as costs or labour inputs, a tendency evident in both rural and urban societies, but especially where industrial and post-industrial methods of production are applied. We encourage efforts to establish managerial and technological conditions that enable workers to participate meaningfully in significant decision-making processes, and to create opportunities for individual development by designing positions that challenge them to develop their potential and by instituting educational programmes.

22. God gives talents to individuals for the benefit of the whole community. Human work should be a contribution to the common good (Ephesians 4:28). The modern drift from concern for community to preoccupation with self, supported by powerful structural and cultural forces, shapes the way we work. Individual self-interest can legitimately be pursued, but only in a context marked by the pursuit of the good of others. These two pursuits are complementary. In order to make the pursuit of the common good possible, Christians need to seek to change both the attitudes of workers and the structures in which they work.

23. Discrimination in work continues to oppress people, especially women and marginalised groups. Because of race and gender, people are often pushed into a narrow range of occupations which are often underpaid, offer little status or security, and provide few promotional

opportunities and fringe benefits. Women and men and people of all races are equal before God and should, therefore, be recognised and treated with equal justice and dignity in social and economic life.

24. For most people work is an arduous good. Many workers suffer greatly under the burden of work. In some situations people work long hours for low pay, working conditions are appalling, contracts are non-existent, sexual harassment occurs, trade union representation is not allowed, health and safety regulations are flouted. These things occur throughout the world whatever the economic system. The word "exploitation" has a strong and immediate meaning in such situations. The God of the Bible condemns exploitation and oppression. God's liberation of the Israelites from their oppression served as a paradigm of how God's people should behave towards workers in their midst (Leviticus 25:39-55).

25. Since work is central to God's purpose for humanity, people everywhere have both the obligation and the right to work. Given the broad definition of work suggested above (cf. para 13), the right to work here should be understood as part of the freedom of the individual to contribute to the satisfaction of the needs of the community. It is a freedom right, since work in its widest sense is a form of self-expression. The right involved is the right of the worker to work unhindered. The obligation is on every human being to contribute to the community. It is in this sense that Paul says, "if a man will not work, let him not eat."

26. The right to earn a living would be a positive or sustenance right. Such a right implies the obligation of the community to provide employment opportunities. Employment cannot be guaranteed where rights conflict and resources may be inadequate. However the fact that such a right cannot be enforced does not detract in any way from the obligation to seek the highest level of employment which is consistent with justice and the availability of resources.

Rest and Leisure

27. As the Sabbath commandment indicates, the Biblical concept of rest should not be confused with the modern concept of leisure. Leisure consists of activities that are ends in themselves and therefore intrinsically enjoyable. In many parts of the world for many people, life is "all work and no play." While masses of people are unemployed and thus

have only "leisure," millions of people — including children — are often overworked simply to meet their basic survival needs. Meanwhile, especially in economically developed nations, many overwork to satisfy their desire for status.

28. The first pages of the Bible tell us that God rested after creating the universe (Genesis 2:2-3). The sequence of work and rest that we see in God's activity is a pattern for human beings. In that the Sabbath commandment interrupted work with regular periods of rest, it liberates human beings from enslavement to work. The Sabbath erects a fence around human productive activity and serves to protect both human and non-human creation. Human beings have, therefore, both a right and an obligation to rest.

29. Corresponding to the four basic relations in which all people stand (in relationship to non-human creation, to themselves, to other human beings, and to God), there are four activities which we should cultivate in leisure time. Rest consists in the enjoyment of nature as God's creation, in the free exercise and development of abilities which God has given to each person, in the cultivation of fellowship with one another, and above all, in delight in communion with God.

30. Worship is central to the Biblical concept of rest. In order to be truly who they are, human beings need periodic moments of time in which God's commands concerning their work will recede from the forefront of their consciousness as they adore the God of loving holiness and thank the God of holy love.

31. Those who cannot meet their basic needs without having to forego leisure can be encouraged by the reality of their right to rest. The right to rest implies the corresponding right to sustenance for all those who are willing to work "six days a week" (Exodus 20:9). Modern workaholics whose infatuation with status relegates leisure to insignificance must be challenged by the liberating obligation to rest. What does it profit them to "gain the whole world" if they "forfeit their life" (Mark 8:36)?

C. Poverty and Justice

God and the Poor

32. Poverty was not part of God's original creation, nor will poverty be part of God's restored creation when Christ returns. Involuntary poverty

in all its forms and manifestations is a result of the Fall and its consequences. Today one of every five human beings lives in poverty so extreme that their survival is daily in doubt. We believe this is offensive and heart breaking to God.

33. We understand that the God of the Bible is one who in mercy extends love to all. At the same time, we believe that when the poor are oppressed, God is the "defender of the poor" (Psalm 146:7-9). Again and again in every part of Scripture, the Bible expresses God's concern for justice for the poor. Faithful obedience requires that we share God's concern and act on it. "He who oppresses a poor man insults his maker, but he who is kind to the needy honours Him" (Proverbs 14:31). Indeed it is only when we right such injustices that God promises to hear our prayers and worship (Isaiah 58:1-9).

34. Neglect of the poor often flows from greed. Furthermore, the obsessive or careless pursuit of material goods is one of the most destructive idolatries in human history (Ephesians 5:5). It distracts individuals from their duties before God, and corrupts personal and social relationships.

Causes of Poverty

35. The causes of poverty are many and complex. They include the evil that people do to each other, to themselves, and to their environment. The causes of poverty also include the cultural attitudes and actions taken by social, economic, political and religious institutions, that either devalue or waste resources, that erect barriers to economic production, or that fail to reward work fairly. Furthermore, the forces that cause and perpetuate poverty operate at global, national, local, and personal levels. It is also true that a person may be poor because of sickness, mental or physical handicap, childhood, or old age. Poverty is also caused by natural disasters such as earthquakes, hurricanes, floods, and famines.

36. We recognise that poverty results from and is sustained by both constraints on the production of wealth and on the inequitable distribution of wealth and income. We acknowledge the tendency we have had to reduce the causes of poverty to one at the expense of the others. We affirm the need to analyse and explain the conditions that promote the creation of wealth, as well as those that determine the distribution of wealth.

21

37. We believe it is the responsibility of every society to provide people with the means to live at a level consistent with their standing as persons created in the image of God.

Justice and Poverty

38. Biblical justice means impartially rendering to everyone their due in conformity with the standards of God's moral law. Paul uses justice (or righteousness) in its most comprehensive sense as a metaphor to describe God's creative and powerful redemptive love. Christ, solely in grace, brought us into God's commonwealth, who were strangers to it and because of sin cut off from it (Romans 1:17-18; 3:21-26; Ephesians 2:4-22). In Biblical passages which deal with the distribution of the benefits of social life in the context of social conflict and social wrong, justice is related particularly to what is due to groups such as the poor, widows, orphans, resident aliens, wage earners and slaves. The common link among these groups is powerlessness by virtue of economic and social needs. The justice called forth is to restore these groups to the provision God intends for them. God's law expresses this justice and indicates its demands. Further, God's intention is for people to live, not in isolation, but in society. The poor are described as those who are weak with respect to the rest of the community; the responsibility of the community is stated as "to make them strong" so that they can continue to take their place in the community (Leviticus 25:35-36). One of the dilemmas of the poor is their loss of community (Job 22:5; Psalm 107:4-9, 33-36). Indeed their various needs are those that tend to prevent people from being secure and contributing members of society. One essential characteristic of Biblical justice is the meeting of basic needs that have been denied in contradiction to the standards of Scripture; but further, the Bible gives indication of how to identify which needs are basic. They are those essential, not just for life, but for life in society.

39. Justice requires special attention to the weak members of the community because of their greater vulnerability. In this sense, justice is partial. Nevertheless, the civil arrangements in rendering justice are not to go beyond what is due to the poor or to the rich (Deuteronomy 1:17; Leviticus 19:15). In this sense justice is ultimately impartial. Justice is so fundamental that it characterises the personal virtues and personal relationships of individuals as they faithfully follow God's

standards. Those who violate God's standards, however, receive God's retributive justice, which often removes the offender from society or from the divine community.

40. Justice requires conditions such that each person is able to participate in society in a way compatible with human dignity. Absolute poverty, where people lack even minimal food and housing, basic education, health care, and employment, denies people the basic economic resources necessary for just participation in the community. Corrective action with and on behalf of the poor is a necessary act of justice. This entails responsibilities for individuals, families, churches, and governments.

41. Justice may also require socio-political actions that enable the poor to help themselves and be the subjects of their own development and the development of their communities. We believe that we and the institutions in which we participate are responsible to create an environment of law, economic activity, and spiritual nurture which creates these conditions.

Some Urgent Contemporary Issues

42. Inequitable international economic relations aggravate poverty in poor countries. Many of these countries suffer under a burden of debt service which could only be repaid at an unacceptable price to the poor, unless there is a radical restructuring both of national economic policies and international economic relations. The combination of increasing interest rates and falling commodity prices in the early 1980s has increased this debt service burden. Both lenders and borrowers shared in creating this debt. The result has been increasing impoverishment of the people. Both lenders and borrowers must share responsibility for finding solutions. We urgently encourage governments and international financial institutions to redouble their efforts to find ways to reduce the international indebtedness of the Third World, and to ensure the flow of both private and public productive capital where appropriate.

43. Government barriers to the flow of goods and services often work to the disadvantage of the poor. We particularly abhor the protectionist policies of the wealthy nations which are detrimental to developing countries. Greater freedom and trade between nations is an important part of reducing poverty worldwide.

44. Justice requires that the value of money be reliably known and stable, thus inflation represents poor stewardship and defrauds the nations' citizens. It wastes resources and is particularly harmful to the poor and the powerless. The wealthier members of society find it much easier to protect themselves against inflation than do the poor. Rapid changes in prices drastically affect the ability of the poor to purchase basic goods.

45. Annual global military expenditures equal the annual income of the poorest one-half of the world's people. These vast, excessive military expenditures detract from the task of meeting basic human needs, such as food, health care, and education. We are encouraged by the possibilities represented by the changes in the USSR and Eastern Europe, and improving relations between East and West. We urge that a major part of the resulting "peace dividend" be used to provide sustainable solutions to the problems of the world's poor.

46. Drug use and trafficking destroys both rich and poor nations. Drug consumption reflects spiritual poverty among the people and societies in which drug use is apparent. Drug trafficking undermines the national economies of those who produce drugs. The economic, social, and spiritual costs of drug use are unacceptable. The two key agents involved in this problem must change: the rich markets which consume drugs and the poorer countries which produce them. Therefore both must urgently work to find solutions. The rich markets which consume drugs must end their demand. And the poorer countries which produce them must switch to other products.

47. We deplore economic systems based on policies, laws, and regulations whose effect is to favour privileged minorities and to exclude the poor from fully legitimate activities. Such systems are not only inefficient, but are immoral as well in that participating in and benefitting from the formal economy depends on conferred privilege of those who have access and influence to public and private institutions rather than on inventiveness and hard work. Actions need to be taken by public and private institutions to reduce and simplify the requirements and costs of participating in the national economy.

48. There is abundant evidence that investment in small scale enterprises run by and for the poor can have a positive impact upon income and job creation for the poor. Contrary to the myths upheld by traditional financial institutions, the poor are often good entrepreneurs and excellent credit risks. We deplore the lack of credit available to the

poor in the informal sector. We strongly encourage governments, financial institutions, and Non-Governmental Organisations to redouble their efforts to significantly increase credit to the poor. We feel so strongly about this that a separate statement dedicated to credit-based income generation programmes has been issued by the conference.

D. Freedom, Government, and Economics

The Language of Human Rights

49. With the United Nations Declaration of Human Rights, the language of human rights has become pervasive throughout the world. It expresses the urgent plight of suffering people whose humanity is daily being denied them by their oppressors. In some cases rights language has ben misused by those who claim that anything they want is theirs "by right." This breadth of application has led some to reject rights as a concept, stating that if everything becomes a right then nothing will be a right, since all rights imply corresponding responsibilities. Therefore it is important to have clear criteria for what defines rights.

Christian Distinctives

50. All human interaction is judged by God and is accountable to God. In seeking human rights we search for an authority or norm which transcends our situation. God is that authority; God's character constitutes that norm. Since human rights are a priori rights, they are not conferred by the society or the state. Rather, human rights are rooted in the fact that every human being is made in the image of God. The deepest ground of human dignity is that while we were yet sinners, Christ died for us (Romans 5:8).

51. In affirmation of the dignity of God's creatures, God's justice for them requires life, freedom, and sustenance. The divine requirements of justice establish corresponding rights for human beings to whom justice is due. The right to life is the most basic human right. God created human beings as free moral agents. As such, they have the right to freedom — e.g., freedom of religion, speech, and assembly. Their freedom, however, is properly used only in dependence on God. It is a

25

requirement of justice that human beings, including refugees and state-less persons, are able to live in society with dignity. Human beings therefore have a claim on other human beings for social arrangements that ensure that they have access to the sustenance that makes life in society possible.

52. The fact that in becoming Christians we may choose to forego our rights out of love for others and in trust of God's providential care does not mean that such rights cease to exist. Christians may endure the violation of their rights with great courage but work vigorously for the identical rights of others in similar circumstances. However it may not be appropriate to do so in some circumstances. Indeed this disparity between Christian contentment and campaigning on behalf of others in adverse situations is a witness to the work and love of God.

53. All of us share the same aspirations as human beings to have our rights protected — whether the right to life, freedom, or sustenance. Yet the fact of sin and the conflict of competing human rights means that our aspirations are never completely fulfilled in this life. Through Christ, sin and evil have been conquered. They will remain a destructive force until the consummation of all things. But that in no way reduces our horror at the widespread violation of human rights today.

Democracy

54. As a model, modern political democracy is characterised by limited government of a temporary character, by the division of power within the government, the distinction between state and society, pluralism, the rule of law, institutionalisation of freedom rights (including free and regular elections), and a significant amount of non-governmental control of property. We recognise that no political system is directly prescribed by Scripture, but we believe that Biblical values and historical experience call Christians to work for the adequate participation of all people in the decision-making processes on questions that affect their lives.

55. We also recognise that simply to vote periodically is not a sufficient expression of democracy. For a society to be truly democratic economic power must be shared widely and class and status distinctions must not be barriers preventing access to economic and social institutions. Democracies are also open to abuse through the very chances

which make them democratic. Small, economically powerful groups sometimes dominate the political process. Democratic majorities can be swayed by materialistic, racist, or nationalistic sentiments to engage in unjust policies. The fact that all human institutions are fallen means that the people must be constantly alert to and critical of all that is wrong.

56. We recognise that no particular economic system is directly prescribed by Scripture. Recent history suggests that a dispersion of ownership of the means of production is a significant component of democracy. Monopolistic ownership, either by the state, large economic institutions, or oligarchies is dangerous. Widespread ownership, either in a market economy or a mixed system, tends to decentralise power and prevent totalitarianism.

The Concentration of Economic Power

57. Economic power can be concentrated in the hands of a few people in a market economy. When that occurs political decisions tend to be made for economic reasons and the average member of society is politically and economically marginalised. Control over economic life may thus be far removed from a large part of the population. Transnational corporations can also wield enormous influence on some economies. Despite these problems, economic power is diffused within market-oriented economies to a greater extent than in other systems.

58. In centrally planned economies, economic decisions are made for political reasons, people's economic choices are curtailed, and the economy falters. Heavy state involvement and regulation within market economies can also result in concentrations of power that effectively marginalise poorer members of the society. Corruption almost inevitably follows from concentrated economic power. Widespread corruption so undermines society that there is a virtual breakdown of legitimate order.

Capitalism and Culture

59. As non-capitalist countries increasingly turn away from central planning and towards the market, the question of capitalism's effect on

27

culture assumes more and more importance. The market system can be an effective means of economic growth, but can, in the process, cause people to think that ultimate meaning is found in the accumulation of more goods.[The overwhelming consumerism of Western societies is testimony to the fact that the material success of capitalism encourages forces and attitudes that are decidedly non-Christian. One such attitude is the treatment of workers as simply costs or productive inputs, without recognition of their humanity. There is also the danger that the model of the market, which may work well in economic transactions, will be assumed to be relevant to other areas of life, and people may consequently believe that what the market encourages is therefore best or most true.]

The Role of Government

60. Government is designed to serve the purposes of God to foster community, particularly in response to our rebellious nature (Romans 13:1, 4; Psalm 72:1). As an institution administered by human beings, government can exacerbate problems of power, greed, and envy. However, it can, where properly constructed and constrained, serve to limit some of these sinful tendencies. Therefore it is the responsibility of Christians to work for governmental structures that serve justice. Such structures must respect the principle that significant decisions about local human communities are usually best made at a level of government most directly responsible to the people affected.

61. At a minimum, government must establish a rule of law that protects life, secures freedom, and provides basic security. Special care must be taken to make sure the protection of fundamental rights is extended to all members of society, especially the poor and oppressed (Proverbs 31:8-9; Daniel 4:27). Too often government institutions are captured by the economically or socially powerful. Thus, equality before the law fails to exist for those without power. Government must also have regard for economic efficiency and appropriately limit its own scope and action.

62. The provision of sustenance rights is also an appropriate function of government. Such rights must be carefully defined so that government's involvement will not encourage irresponsible behaviour and the breakdown of families and communities. In a healthy society,

this fulfilment of rights will be provided through a diversity of institutions so that the government's role will be that of last resort.

Mediating Structures

63. One of the phenomena associated with the modern world is the increasing divide between private and public sectors. The need for a bridge between these two sectors has led to an emphasis on mediating institutions. The neighbourhood, the family, the church, and other voluntary associations are all such institutions. As the early church did in its context, these institutions provide citizens with many opportunities for participation and leadership. They also provide other opportunities for loyalty in addition to the state and the family. Their role in meeting the needs of members of the community decreases the need for centralised government. They also provide a channel for individuals to influence government, business, and other large institutions. Therefore Christians should encourage governments everywhere to foster vigorous voluntary associations.

64. The future of poverty alleviation is likely to involve expanded microeconomic income generation programmes and entrepreneurial development of the so-called "informal sector" as it becomes part of the transformed formal economy. In this context, there will most likely be an even greater role for Non-Governmental Organisations. In particular, church bodies will be able to make a significant and creative contribution in partnership with the poor, acting as mediating institutions by virtue of the churches' longstanding grass-roots involvement in local communities.

Conclusion

65. As we conclude, we thank God for the opportunity God has given us to participate in this conference. Through our time together we have been challenged to express our faith in the area of economic life in practical ways. We acknowledge that all too often we have allowed society to shape our views and actions and have failed to apply scriptural teaching in this crucial area of our lives, and we repent.

We now encourage one another to uphold Christian economic

values in the face of unjust and subhuman circumstances. We realise, however, that ethical demands are often ineffective because they are reinforced only by individual conscience and that the proclamation of Christian values needs to be accompanied by action to encourage institutional and structural changes which would foster these values in our communities. We will therefore endeavour to seek every opportunity to work for the implementation of the principles outlined in this **Declaration,** in faithfulness to God's calling.

We urge all people, and especially Christians, to adopt stewardship and justice as the guiding principles for all aspects of economic life, particularly for the sake of those who are most vulnerable. These principles must be applied in all spheres of life. They have to do with our use of material resources and lifestyle as well as with the way people and nations relate to one another. With girded loins and burning lamps we wait for the return of our Lord Jesus Christ when justice and peace shall embrace.

PART II

Work and the Gifts of the Spirit[1]

Miroslav Volf

Immediately after it ended, the Oxford Conference on Christian Faith and Economics was described as "historic." This was, no doubt, overly hasty and optimistic. But whatever one decides in the future about the "historic" nature of the conference, there is no doubt that the document on the relationship between Christian faith and economics produced there by more than one hundred theologians, economists, ethicists, development experts, church leaders, and business people — all with allegiances to various traditions of theological and economic thought — is noteworthy.

One of the most difficult challenges of all international theological conferences on social and ethical issues is integration of the various contextually and ideologically conditioned perspectives of the participants. Such conferences are faced with the alternatives of producing a document in which one perspective dominates or of being content with inconsequential platitudes. The inability to mediate between the various perspectives paralyzed, for example, the Conference on Justice, Peace, and the Integrity of Creation in Seoul (1990); the delegates were unable to give a common answer to the great problems of today's world. So the Seoul conference opted for the second alternative, and the disappointment was general.[2] It is the strength of the Oxford Declaration on

1. This chapter is a free translation of a section from "Arbeit, Geist und Schöpfung," in Hermann Sautter and Miroslav Volf, *Gerechtigkeit, Geist und Schöpfung. Die Oxford-Erklärung zur Frage von Glaube und Wirtschaft* (Wuppertal: Brockhaus, 1992), pp. 32-60. Richard Heyduck provided the first draft of the translation.

2. For short and helpful analyses of the conference in Seoul by evangelical

33

Christian Faith and Economics (which was partially conceived of as an evangelical contribution to the ecumenical process on Justice, Peace, and the Integrity of Creation) that it succeeded in transcending this unpleasant alternative.

The success in mediating between opposing positions was most clearly visible in the last two parts of the Oxford Declaration (on "Poverty and Justice" and "Freedom, Government, and Economics"), not least because the great debate between the left and the right was concentrated on these problem areas. But the first two parts of the Oxford Declaration (on "Creation and Stewardship" and "Work and Leisure") are in this respect equally successful. Furthermore, they make significant contributions to theological reflection on work through new and courageous perspectives. The most consequential of these contributions is the abandonment of the traditional Protestant vocational view of work in favor of a pneumatological view of work.

In the following comments I will concentrate primarily on this change of the theological paradigm for understanding work and comment exclusively on the section of the Oxford Declaration entitled "Work and Leisure."

Eschatological and Pneumatological Perspectives

Traditionally, theological reflection on human work has moved principally on the ethical level, dealing chiefly with the relationship between work and sanctification.[3] Two questions have been of special interest: First, what are the implications of the new life in Christ for work? And second, how does work influence Christian character? With respect to the first question one heard, for instance, imperatives to work on behalf of poor neighbors or not to practice certain occupations such as that of

---

authors sympathetic to its goals, see Ronald J. Sider, "Reflections on Justice and Peace and the Integrity of Creation," *Transformation* 7, no. 3 (1990): 15-17; Christopher Sugden, "The Poor Are the Losers," *Transformation* 7, no. 3 (1990): 18-19.

3. In the present article I will refrain from referring to secondary literature. I am drawing on my earlier publications on the relationship between Christian faith and economics: *Work in the Spirit: Toward a Theology of Work* (New York: Oxford, 1991); "Arbeit und Charisma. Zur Theologie der Arbeit," *Zeitschrift für evangelische Ethik* 31 (1987): 411-33; "On Human Work: An Evaluation of the Key Ideas of the Encyclical *Laborem Exercens*," *Scottish Journal of Theology* 36 (1984): 65-79.

a soldier. With respect to the second the need to work in order to control the "bodily passions" was stressed. When theologians ventured a step beyond ethical reflection on work and dealt with its theological significance, they concentrated on the relationship between human work and divine creation. At the time of the Reformation, both Luther and Calvin emphasized that a person is created for work, "like the bird for flying" (Luther), and that God preserves the creation through human work. Humans were created for, among other purposes, cooperation with God through their daily work. This creation-theological reflection on work served as the broad framework for ethical reflection.

The ethical and creation-theological perspectives on work are still dominant in Protestant circles, especially among more conservative Protestants. It is refreshing, therefore, to see the Oxford Declaration place the creation-theological framework *into the broader context of pneumatology and eschatology.* Granted, this document does not pursue ethical and creation-theological reflection consistently from a pneumatological and eschatological perspective; like most consensus documents, the Oxford Declaration is at points inconsistent. Yet the pneumatological and eschatological reflection is definitely taken as the overarching framework for reflection on work. Admittedly, this is how I read the document. One can also read it so that the creation-theological and pneumatological-eschatological perspectives stand unreconciled next to each other. What one cannot do, however, is ignore the latter.

In analyzing the section on "Work and Leisure" I will follow the outline of the document. First, I will discuss briefly the comprehensive definition of work and its anthropological significance. Then I will examine what I see as the central idea of the section, which is the relationship between work and the gifts of the Spirit. From these considerations come important perspectives on the theological significance of work and on alienation in work. I will close with some remarks on leisure. My goal is not only to comment on the document but also to demonstrate the plausibility of its innovative eschatological-pneumatological perspective on work.

What Is Work?

"Work and Leisure" begins with a short definition of work: "Work involves all those activities done, not for their own sake, but to satisfy human needs" (13).[4] Correspondingly leisure is defined as those activities "that are ends in themselves and therefore intrinsically enjoyable" (27). Against both these definitions one could rightfully object that they are too exclusive. Taken strictly they imply that one cannot do work for its own sake and that leisure activities cannot satisfy human needs. This is certainly not the case. We can work because we like working; in fact, the more work is done for its own sake the more humane will it be. Similarly, leisure activities are not done simply for their own sake, but, like various useful hobbies, often serve to meet certain needs that are extrinsic to the leisurely activity itself. The distinction between work and leisure that the Oxford Declaration puts forth only applies when it is qualified: Work serves *primarily* the meeting of needs and leisure activities are *primarily* done for their own sake. This is the notion of work with which the Oxford Declaration itself in fact operates when it states that "work has intrinsic value" and is therefore "not solely a means to an end."

Notwithstanding this sort of vagueness, the simple definition of work that the Oxford Declaration gives is significant, above all because it is sufficiently comprehensive to fit the complex phenomena of work in various societies. In Christian social ethics there is a tendency to reduce work to hired labor. Such a reductive understanding reflects the social developments that resulted from industrialization and places hired labor in the center of human life. But today "working for others" is slowly ceasing to be the dominant form of human work even in industrialized societies. Furthermore, any definition of work that excludes significant human activities from the concept of work is socially oppressive because we attach special value to work and because work gives us access to social power. It is, for example, not simply erroneous but also oppressive to think that what homemakers do is not really work. We need a definition of work that allows us to treat doing laundry no less as work than we treat the shuttling of the satellites in the universe. The Oxford Declaration's definition meets this challenge because it understands as work all activities done (primarily) in order to satisfy human needs.

In order to reach a comprehensive theological understanding of work, we must resist tendencies to restrict the concept of work to *gainful* employment. This restrictive tendency was present as a rule in the

---

4. The numbers in parentheses refer to the paragraphs in the Oxford Declaration.

traditional Protestant conception of work as calling *(vocatio).* In contrast to Luther himself but in faithfulness to the analogy to the one spiritual calling *(vocatio spiritualis),* the Lutheran social ethic concentrated its vocational understanding of work *(vocatio externa)* on career-oriented gainful employment. A pneumatological conception of work built theologically on the *multiple and changing* gifts of the Spirit (see below) rather than on the one and permanent calling of God fits better a broader definition of work.

The Anthropological Significance of Work

After defining work the Oxford Declaration moves on to consider the relationship between work and human nature. On the basis of the first and second creation accounts (Genesis 1:26-28 and 2:15) it asserts that in their work human beings "fulfil an original purpose of the Creator for human existence" (13). Work is therefore more than something human beings do; it is part and parcel of who they are created to *be.* Work is "a noble expression of human creation in the image of God," we read a few paragraphs further on (20). This conception of the anthropological significance of work leads the Oxford Declaration to draw an important conclusion and to issue a significant warning. Both the conclusion and the warning are directed against an understanding of work common in modern industrial and information societies.

Because work is central to the Creator's intention for humanity, it has intrinsic value. "It is not simply a chore to be endured for the sake of satisfying human desires or needs, especially the consumption of goods" (14). This means that *work has a human dignity, and does not merely create economic value.* The implication is that work needs to be done in such a way that human dignity is protected. This requires also structural arrangements that make such work possible.

The Oxford Declaration warns furthermore against overvaluing work. In modern societies work is, paradoxically, not only degraded to a mere means, but at the same time elevated as the key to anthropology and the basis for true human identity. Work decisively shapes human personality, but with regard to human *personhood* — with regard to the core of what they are as God's covenant partners — human beings are not their own products, but the creation of God. The Oxford Declaration states rightly: "The essence of human beings consists in that they are

37

made in the image of God. Their ultimate, but not exclusive, source of meaning and identity does not lie in work, but in becoming children of God by one Spirit through faith in Jesus Christ" (14).

Work and the Gifts of the Spirit

Where one expects the conventional Protestant reflection on work to introduce the concept of calling *(vocatio),* the Oxford Declaration speaks of the *gifts of the Spirit.* "When people respond to the call of God, God enables them to bear the fruit of the Spirit and endows them individually with *multiple gifts of the Spirit.* As those who are gifted by the Spirit and whose actions are guided by the demands of love, Christians should do their work in the service of God and humanity" (15). The theological category with which the Oxford Declaration interprets daily work is therefore not calling *(vocatio, klēsis)* but *charisma* or gift. This is a momentous step, one that finds partial support in Puritan reflection on work. A pneumatological understanding of work retains all the strengths of the Protestant vocational understanding of work[5] (e.g., the conviction that all activities have fundamentally the same value in the sight of God because God calls us to perform them), but also overcomes its significant problems. I will first discuss to what extent the conception of work based on the concept of charism is applicable to modern societies and then in the following sections seek to show how it can be helpful in discussing the meaning of work, in dealing with alienation, and in reflecting on leisure.

First, the traditional Protestant vocational conception of work is not applicable to modern societies in which a lifelong commitment to one occupation has increasingly given place to alternating jobs. According to the vocational conception of work a person receives one calling, which is — in the strict theological sense — "irrevocable." Everyone should therefore remain in the one occupation that they are in. A change of occupation is synonymous with unfaithfulness.

With the pneumatological conception of work this is not the case. One cannot choose one's own charism: It is the Spirit who distributes

---

5. See Lee Hardy, *The Fabric of This World: Inquiries Into Calling, Career Choice, and the Design of Human Work* (Grand Rapids: Eerdmans, 1990), pp. 80ff. See also my debate with Hardy in *Calvin Theological Journal* 29 (April 1994).

the charisms "just as the Spirit chooses" (1 Cor. 12:11). But one can and should still strive after different charisms (see 1 Cor. 12:31; 14:1-12). One can therefore speak of a plurality of charisms that correspond to one's changing occupations and jobs. If a person changes her occupation in correspondence to bestowed charisms, this need not be an expression of unfaithfulness but can be an expression of faithfulness to the prompting of the Spirit.

In analogy to the one spiritual calling *(vocatio spiritualis),* the vocational understanding of work assumes that at one time one can have only one vocation, one occupation. But modern societies are characterized by a plurality of occupations and jobs. A pneumatological understanding of work can deal well with this phenomenon. According to the New Testament a person can have not only sequentially more than one charism, but multiple charisms at one and the same time. With the pneumatological conception of work one can assign "theological dignity" not only to occupational gainful employment but also to other jobs that one does. Since one can have multiple charisms, one can be involved in a synchronic plurality of jobs without having to degrade them as sideline jobs. In a word, a pneumatological understanding of work fits better with dynamic modern societies.

Work as Cooperation with God

The ultimate meaning of work lies in cooperation with God. The Oxford Declaration describes this cooperation first of all with respect to the doctrine of creation: "The deepest meaning of human work is that the almighty God established human work as a means to accomplish God's work in the world. . . . God and human beings are co-labourers in the task of preserving creation" (17). Of course, humans always remain dependent on God. The document stresses this. The document fails to mention, however, God's dependence on humans — probably from needless fear of calling into question God's omnipotence and above all God's aseity.

The Oxford Declaration has, however, no hesitation about speaking not only of the protological but also of the *eschatological* significance of work: "Human work has consequences that go beyond the preservation of creation to the anticipation of the eschatological transformation of the world" (18). The pneumatological perspective makes such understanding of work possible because the Spirit, who gives charisms, is "the first installment" of the eschatological glory (see 2 Cor. 1:22; Rom. 8:23). If it is done in the power of the Spirit, work in which we cooperate with God is active anticipation of the kingdom of God. Of course, this does not mean that humans are building "new heavens and a new earth" (18). In the document there is not a trace of such a naive and arrogant faith in human progress; eschatological salvation is expected from God alone. Nevertheless, humans can make a "small and imperfect contribution" to the emergence of the kingdom of God. As an example of such contribution the Oxford Declaration names the personality structure "of the citizens of the eternal kingdom" (18). What remains unsaid is that God will purify, transfigure, and receive into his eternal kingdom all good and beautiful things that human hands will have created.

One can raise two objections against such an exalted conception of work: It unduly glorifies work and disregards that humans above all work in order to meet their daily needs. The two paragraphs that speak of work as cooperation with God are framed by two other paragraphs that should neutralize these objections. The answer to the second objection consists in the practical stress that "meeting one's needs and the needs of one's community (especially its underprivileged members) [is] an essential purpose of work" (16). The intention behind the conception of work as cooperation with God does not negate this and makes sense only if meeting human needs is interpreted as cooperation with God.

The objection that the understanding of work as cooperation with God excessively glorifies work misses the mark insofar as the document states that "work is not only a means through which the glory of human beings as God's stewards shines forth. It is also a place where the misery of human beings as impeders of God's purpose becomes visible" (19). The notion of work as collaboration with God is not a general theory of work. It does not deny that human work also can be done in cooperation with "evil powers which scheme to ruin God's good creation" (19). The judgment of God will make obvious the ultimate meaninglessness of such work. So "cooperation with God" is not only an interpretation of work but also a critique of work.

Starting with charisms one must see work also as *service* to fellow human beings. It is a consistent characteristic of charisms in the New Testament that they are given for serving others (see 1 Cor. 12:4-5). Furthermore, the pneumatological perspective implies that God does not simply call us to cooperate with God but at the same time inspires us for the task and enables us to accomplish it. God does not simply command us from outside but also inspires us from within. It is in this way that we should participate in God's liberative work in the world.

Work and Alienation

The section on work and alienation emphasizes that the pneumatological understanding of work is not an ideology that glosses over the reality of suffering in work (the longest section of Part B). We read here that work is an "ambiguous reality": It is an expression of human creation in the image of God but at the same time also "a painful testimony to human estrangement from God" (20). Human estrangement from God shows itself in, among other things, the various forms of alienation in work. The fact that humans are created in the image of God to have communion with God is both the critical norm for assessing alienation in work and the motivation for overcoming that alienation.

The first form of alienation to be addressed is the reduction of the worker to "mere means," that is, the tendency "to treat workers merely as costs or labour inputs" (21). This form of alienation has two negative consequences: It limits freedom in decision making and hinders personal development. Against this the Oxford Declaration asserts not only that humans are created as free persons, but also that they are gifted by God: Work "as a fundamental dimension of human existence . . . is a personal activity," and humans should not let their God-given abilities be distorted, but should use them in service for the kingdom of God. Naturally this requires corresponding structural changes in the work process. Here we see again the fruitfulness of the pneumatological perspective on work. According to the vocational conception of work, all work — even repetitive piecework — can be characterized as "wholly divine" (Luther). Hence the temptation to misuse as theology an ideology of work. The pneumatological conception of work assumes that an individual's gifts and abilities correspond to the work that she performs. In serving God and fellow humans abilities may not be ignored or passed over but must be preserved and further developed precisely so that one can effectively do service.

Charisms are given for the benefit of the community. To work only for one's own benefit is to be alienated. True human work is

41

always work for others. In order to work for others we do not need only the "attitudes of workers"; the "structures" as well must not foster selfishness. This stress on persons as well as structures is characteristic of the whole document. Behind this stands the double conviction that problems regarding the person cannot be reduced to the structural and that structural problems cannot be reduced to the personal. It is important also that despite all rightful polemic against work for oneself alone the document does not reject self-interest but seeks to understand self-interest in unity with the search for common good. The two complement each other. Their unity is not simply an expression of anthropological sobriety but is also theologically correct. For the *shalom* of the new creation of God involves a person's own wellbeing as well as the wellbeing of all humanity. Hence it is possible for a person to give himself up for others and in the same act "love himself" (Eph. 5:25-28).

The Oxford Declaration names discrimination and exploitation as two other important forms of alienation. People are immediately affected by these forms of alienation even more strongly than by reduction to means or by the egotistical culture and structure of work. It is appropriate that with respect to discrimination the document highlights the problem of women and marginal groups, those who "are often pushed into a narrow range of occupations which are often underpaid, offer little status or security, and provide few promotional opportunities and fringe benefits" (23). Against this the document emphasizes that "women and men and people of all races are equal before God" and should be treated as equals in social and economic life.

Finally the document addresses the problem of economic "exploitation." The description of the toil of work in the Oxford Declaration goes, however, beyond what is usually called "exploitation" and addresses the larger problem of economic oppression. In any case, it is clearly underlined that the God of the Bible not only condemns oppression but is also a God who frees humans from oppression. This liberating God is the model for the people of God, who are called to struggle to overcome the exploitation and oppression that takes place, as the Oxford Declaration states, in all economic systems. The claim that exploitation and oppression "occur throughout the world and whatever the economic system" does not imply, however, that in economic systems all cats are gray and there are no better or worse economic solutions; it is meant simply as a call to vigilance since no system is perfect in this fallen world.

The Right to Work

Immediately after expressing the conviction that not all structural economic solutions are equally good, the Oxford Declaration addresses the right to work. From the fundamental anthropological significance of work it follows that "people everywhere have both the obligation and the right to work" (25). What the document says about the right to work cannot be classified neatly as belonging either to the left or to the right of the economic and political spectrum. (This searching for the middle course characterizes the document as a whole.) On the one hand the right to work is understood as *a freedom* right. It is "the right of the worker to work unhindered" (25). This aspect of the right to work presupposes the comprehensive definition of work as involving more than gainful employment. It speaks of the freedom of individuals "to contribute to the satisfaction of the needs of the community" (25) and presumably also of one's own needs. This dimension of the right to work is stressed against all forms of bureaucratic state socialism, in which the individual has no freedom to work since the land and all "means of production" are the property of the state.

In addition to the conception of the right to work as a freedom, the Oxford Declaration affirms the right to work as a "positive" right, as a right "to earn a living" (26). Such a right implies "the obligation of the community to provide employment opportunities" (26). The right to work as a positive right is the active dimension of the right to sustenance, which the Oxford Declaration later affirms explicitly. "The right to life is the most basic human right. . . . Human beings therefore have a claim on other human beings for social arrangements that ensure that they have access to the sustenance that makes life in society possible" (51). This positive right to work (as distinct from right to sustenance) does not receive the same urgency as does the freedom to work: "Employment cannot be guaranteed where rights conflict and resources might be inadequate" (26). This, however, does not release society of the obligation "to seek the highest level of employment which is consistent with justice and the availability of resources" (26).

With the affirmation of the right to work a clear message is given concerning the problem of unemployment — as clear a message as one can give without restricting freedom rights to such a degree that one can no longer speak of a democratic political order. "Since work is central to God's purpose for humanity" (25), the state has the obligation to create "space" in which people can meet their own needs and participate actively in the economic process.

Work and Leisure

According to the Oxford Declaration work is only one pole of human existence. The other is rest or leisure. "The sequence of work and rest that we see in God's activity is a pattern for human beings" (28). Correspondingly, leisure activities are understood in contrast to work as those activities that "are ends in themselves and therefore intrinsically enjoyable" (27). Leisure is liberating not in a sense of being a sphere of freedom in contrast to slavery, which one experiences in work, but in the sense that it humanizes work itself. As "a fence around human productive activity" the commandment to rest "liberates human beings from enslavement to work" (28). At the same time it protects nature because it allows for restoration of the integrity of nature that has been disturbed by work.

The Oxford Declaration describes types of leisure activities by referring to the four fundamental relationships in which a person stands: to non-human creation, to oneself, to other humans, and to God. It defines "good leisure" as those activities in these four dimensions of life that are an end in themselves: Good leisure "consists in the enjoyment of nature as God's creation, in the free exercise and development of abilities which God has given to each person, in the cultivation of fellowship with one another, and above all, in delight in communion with God" (29).

The only form of leisure activity that is more closely defined in the declaration is fellowship with God. This is unfortunate but understandable since the relationship with God is the very center of the theological conception of rest. This corresponds to the anthropological and soteriological idea that the true identity of humans consists above all in their "becoming children of God" (14). "In order to be truly who they are, human beings need periodic moments of time in which God's commands concerning their work will recede from the forefront of their consciousness as they adore the God of loving holiness and thank the God of holy love" (30). Significantly, the text does not say that the world and worldly work need to disappear from human consciousness in some religious intoxication of worship. No, worldly work is present also in worship. How could it be absent when work is the *active worship* of God in the world (Rom. 12:1)? But during worship, work stands in the background. What stands in the foreground is the final context of the meaning of work, and that is God, who is celebrated in worship.

The relation to the Holy Spirit is not explicit in the Oxford Declaration's reflection on leisure and its relation to work. It is, however, not difficult to show how what is said easily fits a pneumatological perspective. Because *charisma* — gift — serves Paul as a generic term for both liturgical activities (for example, prayer) and daily tasks, it encompasses both rest and work. It makes it possible to understand rest and work as two genuinely interdependent activities. Work is not the only purpose of rest: Rest is intrinsically valuable even though one of its functions is to enrich and ennoble work. And rest is not the only purpose of work: Work is intrinsically meaningful even though it also makes rest possible.

I found the section of the Oxford Declaration on work and leisure biblically and theologically responsible and sensitive to the nature and problems of contemporary societies. But I did not need to be persuaded in the first place because I share its basic approach. In any case, the true success of this section and of the document as a whole will not be measured by whether it persuades theologians but by whether the people of God find in it guidance and inspiration as they go about doing their daily work. They should give it a try. This is the least one must say about the Oxford Declaration.

Credit-Based Income Generation for the Poor

Joe Remenyi and Bill Taylor

In discussions of malnutrition and global starvation it is acknowledged that the world no longer has a food problem. There is more than enough food to feed everyone on the planet more than adequately. Nonetheless, the role of poverty as a root cause of hunger is not given the attention it deserves. Global hunger persists not because there is not enough food to go around, but because the malnourished do not have the wherewithal to buy the food they need. Hence the critical place of income generation. Why then has there been such a serious lack of attention to credit-based income generation programs targeted at investors in the poverty economy? There are many answers to this question but we offer four reasons that our research in this area has identified as important.

The Poverty Cringe

It is still not uncommon to experience the "poverty cringe," especially in official circles, when one suggests working with the poor in the Two-Thirds World. The automatic reaction is to list, consciously or unconsciously, the problems that will have to be dealt with because the poor are "illiterate, itinerant, and unaccountable." The stock response is to deny the poor the respect and recognition that one does not think twice about giving to a clean, well-dressed engineer, agronomist, teacher, or doctor. "The idea that the poor are themselves ultimately responsible for the backwardness and lack of progress in rural areas of the Two Thirds World is not only fairly widely accepted in Western

46

nations but also reflects a prevalent trend of thinking among the ruling elite of the developing world."[1]

Chronic poverty is a symptom of the existence of systems of injustice in our societies. No matter how much one wishes to avoid the rhetoric of the bleeding heart do-gooder fraternity, the reality is that the poor are victims of entrenched socioeconomic systems that allow poverty to persist. There is no evidence that the poor want to be poor. Nor does the evidence of literally thousands upon thousands of small enterprise loan transactions indicate that the poor are less trustworthy or less likely to react in a manner consistent with rational self-interest than are wealthier and better educated persons. The poor deserve our trust and respect as business experts in their own environments. They do not need our charity or patronizing advice.

But the unconscious social biases and prejudices that underlie the "poverty cringe" are very real and primary reasons why it is so easy to fall into the trap of working *for* the poor rather than *with* the poor. David Korten summarizes thus: "In the name of helping the poor, the bureaucracies through which most development assistance is dispensed serve first their own members and then the local elites."[2] Poverty alleviation will not work as a foundation stone of Two-Thirds World development unless the poor are genuinely accorded the respect and dignity they deserve as rational contributors to economic activity in developing countries.

"The Poor Are a Poor Credit Risk"

Western banking practices and prejudices are the basis on which financial systems have developed in the Two-Thirds World. In no area is this more evident than in the rules relating to the borrower's responsibility to furnish the lender with collateral. These rules discriminate against the poor, who have no collateral, and are applied with rigid faith in the theory that it is riskier to lend to the asset-poor than

1. Bertrand Schnieder, *The Barefoot Revolution: A Report to the Club of Rome* (London: Intermediate Technology, 1988), p. 140.
2. David C. Korten, "Third Generation NGO Strategies: A Key to People-Centered Development," *World Development* 15, Supplement (1987): 145-59, here p. 146.

the asset-rich. This faith is applied irrationally, with no apparent thought of whether the repayment record of the poor is as bad as it is assumed to be.[3] Consequently, formal banking systems in the Two-Thirds World do not serve the financial needs of the poor. They do not want to because, presumably, they believe it would be bad for their profitability to do so.

It would be foolhardy to suggest that lending to the poor is not risky. Any form of lending activity carries risks, but the available evidence shows that it is no more risky to lend to the poor than to the rich. If one relies on records of on-time repayment rates, the number of investment loans that must be rescheduled because of difficulty to repay, and default rates for micro-loans of $100 or less compared to commercial banking loans, the opposite is unequivocally the case. An official in Sri Lanka related that the on-time repayment rate on govern-ment-guaranteed loans in that country averaged not more than seven percent in the 1980s. This compares to an average on-time repayment rate on the $1.8 billion of micro-investment loans examined in *Where Credit Is Due*[4] that exceeds ninety percent! This gives us reason to believe that there is profit to be had in helping the poor help them-selves.[5] Yet the poor continue to be denied access to formal credit channels, and this is justified by a persistent belief that the poor are a poor credit risk.

3. See Jack Croucher and S. K. Gupta, "Venture Capital for Microenterprise Development: The VCAT Model," a paper presented at the World Conference on Support of Microenterprises of the Committee of Donor Agencies for Small Enterprise Development, Washington, D.C., June 6-9, 1988; Clyde H. Farnsworth, "Micro-Loans to the World's Poorest," *New York Times,* February 21, 1988; Malcolm Harper and Tan Thiam Soon, *Small Enterprises in Developing Countries* (London: Intermediate Tech-nology, 1979); Jacob Levitsky and Ranga N. Prasad, *Credit Guarantee Schemes for Small and Medium Enterprises* (World Bank Technical Paper 58, Industry and Finance Series; Washington: World Bank, 1987).

4. Joe Remenyi, *Where Credit Is Due* (London: Intermediate Technology, 1991).

5. See Jeffrey Ashe, ed., *The Pisces 11 Experience* I: *Local Efforts in Micro-Enterprise Development.* II: *Local Efforts in Micro-Enterprise Development: Case Studies from Dominican Republic, Costa Rica, Kenya and Egypt* (Washington: USAID, 1985); Bruce R. Bolnick, "Financial Liberalization with Imperfect Markets: Indonesia during the 1970s," *Economic Development and Cultural Change,* April 1987, pp. 581-99; Michael Farbman, ed., *The Pisces Studies: Assisting the Smallest Economic Activi-ties of the Poor* (Washington: USAID, 1981); Norton Jacobi, "Loan Principles that Have Worked in Sri Lanka," *Together,* January-March 1988, p. 7.

"The Poor Are Stuck in a Poverty Trap"

In a similar vein, it is commonly held that the poor remain poor because they are stuck in a poverty trap. The trap is sustained because there is a lack of profitable investment opportunities available to the poor. Only the big push of a government-backed integrated development program can, it is thought, overcome the depressed economic condition of the poor, which causes poverty to be chronic. The poverty trap thesis has enshrined the notion that poverty is too big a problem for anything but government intervention to overcome.

The poverty trap is also characterized in the conventional wisdom by low productivity, which keeps wages low and demand for commodities modest. Low incomes entrench the depressed state of the poor, scotching any possibility that survival-level incomes might form the basis of a demand-led escape from poverty initiated from within the private sector. What is more, because incomes are so low, the poor are perceived as being unable to accumulate adequate savings to finance viable business ventures.

But anecdotal evidence and what data there are on how the poor survive, what they do to earn their incomes, and what they do with their incomes contradict the conclusions suggested by the poverty trap thesis.[6] Average productivity in enterprises run by the poor is low, but the response of productivity to even quite small investments can be dramatic. Demand for commodities by the poor is also highly sensitive to income changes, so that the multiplier effect on growth in income from strategic "pump priming" in support of income and employment generation projects can be very large. And the poor do save, but in very small amounts at any one time. The challenge for operators of credit-based income generation programs (and for borrowers from such programs) is to find ways to ensure that these savings are utilized and effectively invested, without imposing procedures and bureaucratic niceties that generate excessive transaction costs. If the poor can be provided with an outlet for their savings that will reward their frugality with a positive real rate of return, a great step will have been taken to destroy the conditions that make poverty a trap for so many in the world today.

6. See S. V. Sethuraman, ed., *The Urban Informal Sector in Developing Countries* (Geneva: ILO, 1981), especially pp. 29-36.

"What Is Good for the Nation Is Good for the Poor"

Government development projects are, in the main, macroeconomic in their design and dependent on ripple effects — the trickle-down of benefits — for their impact on poverty. Moreover, the appropriate role of government is often clouded by statements such as, "what is good for the nation is good for the poor." In fact, although government-sponsored economic growth initiatives in the formal modern economy in Two-Thirds World countries can be unequivocally good for the nation, the benefits of economic growth in the modern sector of poor economies largely bypasses those who find their livelihood in the survival enterprises of the poor.

The benefits of economic growth in the formal economy tend to bypass the poor because modern sector development projects, even those that are designated as projects of national significance, do so little to improve the productivity of the poor. A new power plant, a new hospital, improved seaport facilities, a new airport terminal, or a new timber mill may augment the standard of living of bureaucrats, captains of industry, skilled workers, and professionals in the formal workforce, but they will barely make a difference to the value-added generated by the firms that employ the poor, produce for the poor, and sell to the poor.

Where Credit Is Due

If we are really serious about abolishing starvation and malnutrition, we have to do much more about reducing poverty. For this to occur we must challenge and reject these fallacies. It is because they hold such a sway that the global commitments of national governments and international agencies to international economic development have not achieved greater inroads in the war on want. We do not understand the problem of poverty because of the myopia of the received wisdom about poverty, which has denied resources to microenterprise development and credit-based poverty alleviation programs. Why are such programs not recognized as alternative "engines of economic growth and development" in the Two-Thirds World?

It is with these questions in mind that we set down here some of the findings of a major study done of credit-based income generation programs across the world, recently published under the title *Where Credit Is Due.*[7]

The Seeds of Success

The seeds of a successful credit-based income generation program are identified as:

- putting people first,
- working *with* the poor instead of *for* the poor,
- the combined discipline of market forces, individual self-interest, and peer group acclaim, support, and discipline, and
- rejection of modernization as the primary goal of development.

Modernization is what must "percolate up" through the "poverty pyramid" if the real income, productivity, and value added of those in poverty is to increase. This means choosing development priorities that

- reduce the price of wage goods,
- reduce unemployment,
- let markets work more effectively to reduce monopoly power,
- do not distort national priorities in a way that cripples the capacity of the economy to meet domestic basic human needs first, and
- promote conditions conducive to broad-based prosperity that includes "prosperity for the poor."

The Client Group

Most of the people of the Two-Thirds World are poor, through no choice of their own. Women and children account for the majority of persons in poverty. The poor are a heterogeneous group that can be characterized as forming a "poverty pyramid." This pyramid persists because poverty has become "systemic" and institutionalized by the constraints that prevent the poor from "raising themselves out of poverty." Credit-based income generation programs for the very poor can break these constraints.

7. See n. 4 above.

The numbers added to the world's poor each year continue to exceed the number that manage to escape from poverty. Consequently, the pace and scale of credit-based investment programs for the poor must be multiplied many times over if the rate of growth of poverty is to be reversed. Nongovernmental organizations are critical in this process because so much official development assistance, despite the rhetoric to the contrary, is reliant on the bankrupt currency of the trickle-down economy. Unless we work directly with the poor we will not succeed in inverting the poverty pyramid. Nothing less is needed.

The Critical Importance of Productivity

The report argues that poverty alleviation has failed because too little attention has been paid in development to raising the productivity of the poor and the value-added produced in the "poverty economy." Social welfare and well-intentioned charity does not alleviate poverty on a sustained basis because they do nothing to augment the productivity of the poor. Credit-based income generation projects that are successful are so because they do not fail in this regard. They generate jobs because the increase in productivity and improved demand for the output of microenterprises make it profitable for employers to take on additional labor. One of the critical constraints that acts to prevent the demand for labor from increasing is the lack of investment finance available to the firms that provide the bulk of the employment of the poor. Credit-based investments in the microenterprises of the poor are a response to this critical constraint and must be evaluated in terms of their impact on productivity and value-added coming from the survival activities of the poor.

The conventional macroeconomic approach to development has failed the poor because it has embraced the notion that development means modernization. Modernization in the formal economy does little to improve the productivity of the poor in the "poverty economy." Moreover, modernization has driven policies that have sucked resources from the traditional economy, exacerbating the deprivation and austerity faced by the poor. This has prevented the poor from investing in their own betterment.

The conventional wisdom in development has also failed the poor because it is based on some critical but fallacious propositions. The poor are not perceived as a potential engine of economic growth because they are seen as a poor risk, untrustworthy, and stuck in a poverty trap characterized by a lack of investment opportunities. The data presented in *Where Credit Is Due* contradicts each of these propositions.

The Evidence

The analysis presented in *Where Credit Is Due* gives evidence from programs that were visited and that account together for $US118,000,000 in loans, the average size of which was less than $100. Supporting evidence is also presented from programs reported in the literature loaning a further $US1,500,000,000 to microenterprises for income generation purposes. The financial results for the typical loan can be summarized as follows:

- The permanent income of borrowers increased by not less than 25 percent,
- jobs were created at a rate of one continuing wage-paying job for every $1000 or less loaned, which is only one-tenth the typical cost of job creation programs in the modern sector of Two-Thirds World economies,
- on-time repayment rates were better than twice that in commercial financial markets in these countries,
- default rates were minimal, and
- estimated social rates of return were typically much greater than those calculated for investments in the modern sector.

Credit-based income generation programs are an important way in which poverty alleviation can be made an effective strategy of economic development. This affirms the importance of economic growth if poverty alleviation is to succeed, but directs our attention to the sort of economic growth that is required.

Conclusions and Policy Implications

There is sufficient evidence to indicate that investment in the enterprises of the poor is well below socially desirable levels. Underinvestment has arisen because development and government policies generally have ignored the informal poverty economy in favor of the formal modern sector. Official development policies have biased the cost of capital to the modern sector below its true social opportunity cost. This has encouraged the substitution of capital for labor and has forcibly channeled the savings of the poor into modern sector applications. Moreover, there is a serious market failure operating insofar as investment decisions in Two-Thirds World economies are based on the misinformation that exists about investment opportunities and risks of lending to the poor. Lending to the poor is good business.

Poverty-targeted development strategies must harness the atomistic nature of competition in the survival economy of the poor. Poverty alleviation policies must tap the vitality and potential of the private enterprise driven economic goals of the thousands on thousands of small businesses that employ and service the consumption needs of the poor.

Public investment in an improved infrastructure servicing the informal economy is important, especially where this influences the health and nutrition of the poor. Also important is the deregulation of markets to allow market forces to operate and to encourage entrepreneurship at all levels of the poverty pyramid. Particular attention must be directed at areas of the economy where monopoly power is vested in the hands of the few. Where these few are public officials administering a government program or semi-independent paragovernment enterprise, there exists a special responsibility to examine whether the continued existence of that monopoly advances or hinders the cause of poverty alleviation in the nation.

The overwhelming importance of private enterprise in the informal poverty economy gives nongovernmental organizations a special place and a special opportunity to take the lead in income and employment generation initiatives among the poor. They have developed a track record that is enviable and give a clear pointer to the future. It is critical that there be more of the same. It is also critical that replication and expansion programs should benefit from the lessons of those that have gone afore.

There are three areas into which this latter challenge will lead. First, the links between the informal poverty economy and the rest of the economy (e.g., more effective links between self-help groups and banks) must improve, especially as this bears on access to loans. This may require existing or yet-to-be-established institutions to develop bridges that allow formal modern sector institutions to service the needs of the poor effectively and efficiently.

Second, if Christian organizations are to become as important as bridges between the poor and the formal economy as they are capable of becoming, they must become risktakers and institutional innovators by seeking to experiment with the creation of new lines of credit for the poor, borrowing on behalf of the clients that they serve from the banks to which the poor now have no access. However, before many of these agencies are able to do this successfully, they will themselves have to become more professional.

Third, greater attention must be given to the impact of government policies on the performance of microenterprises in the poverty economy. Private entrepreneurs operate in a macroeconomic environment, whether rich or poor. In the past, however, microenterprise entrepreneurs have been given little or no consideration in the formulation of macroeconomic or industry policies and priorities. For example, inflation is by far the worst enemy of the poor. If you have very little money, even a little inflation can quickly take what little you have. Yet, few developing countries consider their macroeconomic priorities in these terms. It is similar with industry policy. Although we know that firms in a vibrant sector of the economy fare better than those in a stagnant or declining sector, few Two-Thirds World governments choose economic priorities so as to ensure that the economic cards are stacked in favor of those industries that provide the bulk of the nonfarm employment for the poor.

Until quite recently, development for the poor had dropped off the agenda of most developing countries. Consequently, the informal poverty economy has been ignored as a source of development potential and investment opportunities. Yet, the poor are more than a source of cheap labor and sequestered savings; they are also demanders of the fruits of development and unsatiated consumers of the output of firms in both modern and traditional industries in the economy. It is in the interest of all those who seek economic development and alleviation of poverty to put "development for the poor" back onto the policy agenda in a big way. Credit-based investment programs targeted at the poor are one effective way in which this agenda can become more than barren rhetoric.

Christian organizations have been at the forefront as pioneers in the credit-based income generation field. They are, therefore, in a unique position to ensure that the level of resources devoted to them is increased significantly. Moreover, it is critical that they not wait for some other group to take the lead in doing this. This is our opportunity to ensure that "development through poverty alleviation" is given the priority that is required if the rate of growth of poverty is to be reversed within our lifetime.[8]

8. On the concerns of this chapter see also Charles Elliott, *Comfortable Compassion* (London: Hodder and Stoughton, 1987); David C. Korten, *NGOs and the Future of Asian Development* (Boston: Institute for Development Research, 1988); World Bank, *World Development Report* (Washington: World Bank, 1987).

Justice and Poverty:
Two Views Contrasted

E. Calvin Beisner

The Oxford Declaration on Christian Faith and Economics tells us that "Biblical justice means *impartially* rendering to everyone their *due* in *conformity with the standards* of God's moral law" (38, emphasis added). While there is a sense in which "justice is partial" because it "requires special attention to the weak members of the community because of their greater vulnerability," the Declaration adds, "Nevertheless, the civil arrangements in rendering justice are not to go beyond what is due to the poor or to the rich (Deuteronomy 1:17; Leviticus 19:15). In this sense justice is ultimately impartial" (39).

Immediately following the first quotation above, the Declaration offers another view of justice: "Paul uses justice (or righteousness) in its most comprehensive sense as a metaphor to describe God's creative and powerful redemptive love. Christ, solely in grace, brought us into God's commonwealth, who were strangers to it and because of sin cut off from it (Romans 1:17-18; 3:21-26; Ephesians 2:4-22)" (38). Later the Declaration says that

> Justice requires conditions such that each person is able to participate in society in a way compatible with human dignity. Absolute poverty, where people lack even minimal food and housing, basic education, health care, and employment, denies people the basic economic resources necessary for just participation in the community. Corrective action with and on behalf of the poor is a necessary act of justice. (40)

The thesis of this chapter is that the Declaration thus presents two

57

mutually inconsistent views of justice and that the former is biblical and the latter unbiblical.

The Views Are Mutually Inconsistent

The first view of justice focuses on impartiality, on what is deserved, and on conformity with fixed and definable standards. The second focuses on love, inclusion in the community, and meeting people's needs. As complementary values to be expressed by actions both inside and outside the church, the views are consistent. But as views of *justice,* they are incompatible. Comparison of the criteria that the two views are focused on makes this clear.

The first view calls for impartiality in civil arrangements, exemplified by impartial application of rules to rich and poor alike; the second calls for "conditions such that each person is able to participate in society in a way compatible with human dignity," and it denies that what it calls "absolute poverty" fills those conditions. But if historical reality is that some people live in "absolute poverty," not because others oppress them but because they think and behave in economically unproductive ways, providing "minimal food and housing, basic education, health care, and employment," "just participation in the community" will require partiality in their favor.

The first view calls for rendering to each what is due, recognizing the principle of what is deserved; the second, for providing particular material and social goods without reference to what is deserved. The first view readily comports with Paul's command that whoever refuses to work must not be permitted to eat (2 Thess. 3:10); the second stumbles at such words. It is tempting to surmise that the second view *assumes* that considerations of what is deserved should temper its otherwise untempered demands. But to infer this is to ignore the evidence of the text of the Declaration and its history. Not only does this immediate passage mention no conditions on the provision of these economic goods, which cost someone something even if they do not cost their recipients, but other passages also do the same. Thus we read: "God's intention is for people" — and "people" is unqualified here — "to live, not in isolation, but in society" (38).[1] Furthermore,

---

1. Scripture places conditions on people living in society. See, for instance, instruc-

In affirmation of the dignity of God's creatures, God's justice for them requires life, freedom, and sustenance. The divine requirements of justice establish corresponding rights for human beings to whom justice is due. . . . It is a requirement of justice that human beings . . . are able to live in society with dignity. Human beings therefore have a claim on other human beings for social arrangements that ensure that they have access to the sustenance that makes life in society possible. (51)

Here, again, the references to people ("them," "human beings") and their "claim" on others are unqualified. Significantly, paragraph 37, which in the final version says, "We believe it is the responsibility of every society to provide people with the means to live at a level consistent with their standing as persons created in the image of God," omits an important qualification that appeared in an earlier draft: "We believe it is the responsibility of every society to provide people *who cannot work with no fault of their own* with the means. . . ." That these claims are unqualified, that is, that no conditions are placed on these rights, indicates that the notion of justice put forth in the second sentence of paragraph 38, clarified by paragraph 70 of the first draft of the Composite Discussion Document[2] and the essay on which the

---

tions to "cut off" from the community those who commit various sins or become ceremonially unclean (Exod. 12:15 [cf. v. 19]; 23:23; 30:33, 38; Lev. 7:20f., 25, 27; Exod. 31:14; Lev. 17:3f., 9f., 14; 18:29; 19:8; 20:2f.; 22:24; 23:29; Num. 9:13; 15:30f.; 19:13, 20).

2. The Composite Discussion Document provided the outlines for discussion during the Oxford Conference. Paragraph 70 of its first draft included the following relevant material:

The meaning of justice . . . must be found in the core of what the Christian faith is. At the centre of the Christian faith there is the affirmation that in Christ we encounter the grace of God. In Christ our alienation from God and to each other is overcome. The gift of God's love draws us into community. The barriers which divide people have been brought down in Christ (cf. Eph. 2). It is often thought that God's grace needs to be balanced with God's justice as if they are somehow in tension with one another. This is the case wherever Christians speak of God's justice needing to be satisfied before we can speak of love. But Paul says we are loved despite our unrighteousness.

The separation of love and justice is false. . . .

So, what love desires, justice demands. God's grace is not in contrast to God's justice; God's grace is what defines God's justice. And by God's grace what is due to us . . . is to belong. To belong to God, and to one another.

latter was based,[3] dominates these considerations.

⌐So the first view appeals to definable, unchanging standards, God's moral law, to govern how we determine what is due to everyone; the second sets forth vague, general, and culturally relative measures of material and social goods as due to everyone without condition. For instance, its definition of "absolute poverty" is both problematically imprecise and historically myopic. What, for instance, is "basic education" (40), and what proportion of people has enjoyed it in any given human society through the millennia? Are we to understand "health care" as qualified by "minimal" or "basic" or as unqualified? In any case, what does it include and exclude? Are "minimal" and "basic" to be defined relative to what is common in the late-twentieth-century United States, or what existed in the mid-nineteenth-century United States, or medieval Europe, or Israel under Solomon (e.g., 1 Kgs. 10:21, 27), or Samaria a century later (2 Kgs. 6:24-29), or any of a thousand other societies and economic conditions we might name, ancient and modern? If the standards are defined relative to common conditions in particular geopolitical entities, what happens to the biblical insistence that justice know no boundaries and play no favorites between citizens and aliens? The reciprocity of commutative justice[4] inherent in the first view disarms the problem of cultural relativism; the second view cannot escape cultural relativism.

The Biblical Vocabulary of Justice

Several Hebrew and Greek words are prominent in the biblical material on justice. Because the need for brevity precludes a thorough word study, we must make do here with merely listing the key words, their meanings,[5] and (in footnotes) some of their more significant and illustrative instances.

3. The material was based on (and often repeated word for word) J. Philip Wogaman's paper "Toward a Christian Definition of Justice," delivered at the Regional Conference on Economics and Christianity, sponsored by the Oxford Conference on Christian Faith and Economics, at Wheaton College, February 24-25, 1989, and published in *Transformation* 7, no. 2 (April/June 1990): 18-23.

4. See below on the meaning and application of "commutative justice."

5. The brief definitions here are adapted from Francis Brown, S. R. Driver, and Charles A. Briggs, ed., *A Hebrew and English Lexicon of the Old Testament* (Oxford:

The Hebrew noun-adjective *yāšar*[6] means "straight, right, pleasing (to God or humans), straightforward, just, upright," "the right, right things, the upright; uprightness." *Mišpāṭ*[7] means "judgment," that is, the act, place, process, case, or cause of judgment, "sentence, decision; execution or time of judgment; justice, right, rectitude (of God or humans); ordinance; decision of the judge in a case of law; legal right, privilege, or due." These words correspond closely with Greek *krima*[8] ("dispute, lawsuit; decision, decree; judging or judgment; judicial verdict; sentence of condemnation; pronunciation of judgment") and *krisis*[9] ("judging, judgment; judgment against a person; condemnation [or the punishment that follows]; right, justice, righteousness").

The Hebrew verb *yāšar*[10] means "be smooth, straight, or right; go straight; be pleasing, agreeable, right; ethically, be straightforward, upright; make smooth, straight; lead straight along, direct; esteem right, approve." Hebrew *šāpaṭ*[11] means "judge, govern; act as lawgiver, judge,

---

Clarendon, 1907) for Hebrew words, and from Walter Bauer, *A Greek-English Lexicon of the New Testament and Other Early Christian Literature,* 2d ed., trans. William F. Arndt and F. Wilbur Gingrich, rev. F. Wilbur Gingrich and Frederick W. Danker (Chicago: University of Chicago, 1979) for Greek words.

6. *Yāšar* occurs in Exod. 15:26; Deut. 6:18; 1 Sam. 12:23; 29:6; 1 Kgs. 15:5; 2 Chr. 29:34; Ezra 8:21; Neh. 9:13; Job 1:1; Pss. 7:10; 19:8; 25:8; 33:4; 119:137; 125:4; Prov. 11:3; 14:12; Jer. 31:9; Mic. 3:9. (This and the following lists of uses of the Hebrew and Greek words are illustrative only, not necessarily exhaustive.)

7. *Mišpāṭ* occurs in Gen. 18:19, 25; Exod. 21:1; 23:6; Lev. 18:4f.; 19:15, 35; Num. 27:5; Deut. 1:17; 4:1, 5, 8; 16:18f.; 17:8-11; 24:17; 1 Sam. 8:3; 2 Sam. 8:15; 15:2, 4, 6; 1 Kgs. 8:4, 49; 10:9; Pss. 1:5; 9:4, 7, 16; 72:1f.; 99:4; 103:6; Prov. 21:3; Eccl. 5:8; Isa. 1:21; 28:17, 26; 56:1; 59:8-15; Ezek. 45:9; Amos 5:7, 15, 24; Mic. 6:8; 7:9.

8. *Krima* occurs in Matt. 7:2; 23:14; Mark 12:40; Luke 20:47; 23:40; 24:20; John 9:39; Acts 24:25; Rom. 2:2f.; 3:8; 5:16; 11:33; 13:2; 1 Cor. 6:7; 11:29, 34; Gal. 5:10; 1 Tim. 3:6; 5:12; Heb. 6:2; Jas. 3:1; 1 Pet. 4:17; 2 Pet. 2:3; Jude 1:4; Rev. 17:1; 18:20; 20:4.

9. *Krisis* occurs in Matt. 5:21f.; 10:15; 11:22, 24; 12:18, 20, 36, 41f.; 23:23, 33; Mark 3:29; 6:11; Luke 10:14; 11:31f., 42; John 3:19; 5:22, 24, 27, 29f.; 7:24; 8:16; 12:31; 16:8, 11; Acts 8:33; 2 Thess. 1:5; 1 Tim. 5:24; Heb. 9:27; 10:27; Jas. 2:13; 2 Pet. 2:4, 9, 11; 3:7; 1 John 4:17; Jude 1:6, 9, 15; Rev. 14:7; 16:7; 18:10; 19:2.

10. *Yāšar* occurs in Num. 23:27; 1 Sam. 6:12; 1 Chr. 13:4; Pss. 5:8; 119:128; Prov. 4:25; 11:5; Isa. 45:2.

11. *Šāpaṭ* occurs in Gen. 19:9; Exod. 18:16; Deut. 1:16; 16:18; 25:1; Judg. 3:10; Ruth 1:1; 1 Sam. 8:20; 24:15; 2 Sam. 18:19, 31; 1 Kgs. 3:9; 1 Chr. 16:33; Pss. 7:8; 10:18; 26:1; 43:1; 51:4; 82:3; 96:13; 98:9; Isa. 1:17; 11:4; Ezek. 34:20-24; 36:19.

or governor; decide a controversy; execute judgment by discriminating (between right and wrong, good and bad, true and false, innocent and guilty), vindicating, condemning, or punishing; enter into controversy, plead." These words correspond closely with Greek *krinō*,[12] "separate, distinguish; select, prefer; judge, think, consider; look upon so as to assess; decide, propose, intend; (in law) judge, decide, hale before a court, condemn, hand over for punishment; condemn, administer justice, punish; see that justice is done; pass personal (not legal) judgment, express an opinion (usually an unfavorable opinion) about."

Hebrew *ṣaddîq*[13] means "just, righteous (of governments, God, judges, laws); right (in one's cause, in conduct and character, ethically); justified and vindicated by God; right, correct, lawful." The noun *ṣedeq*[14] denotes "righteousness; what is right, just, or normal (i.e., consistent with a norm or standard); righteousness (in government, of rulers, law, the Davidic king, Jerusalem as seat of government, of God); justice (in a case or cause); rightness (in speech); ethical righteousness; righteousness as vindicated, justification in a controversy; deliverance, victory, prosperity." *Ṣedāqâ*[15] is "righteousness (in government, of a judge, ruler, or king, of law, of the messiah, as an attribute of God administering justice or punishment or in vindicating God's people, in a case or cause); truthfulness; ethical righteousness; righteousness as vindication, justification, salvation; righteous acts." These Hebrew words correspond closely to Greek *dikaiosynē*,[16] "uprightness, justice (of a judge); moral and religious

---

12. *Krinō* occurs in Matt. 5:40; 7:1f.; 19:28; Luke 6:37; 7:43; 12:57; 19:22; 22:30; John 3:17f.; 5:22, 30; 7:24, 51; 8:15f., 26, 50; 12:47f.; 16:11; 18:31; Acts 3:13; 4:19; 7:7; 13:27, 46; 15:19; 16:4, 15; 17:31; 20:16; 21:25; 23:3, 6; 24:6, 21; 25:9, 10, 25; 26:6, 8; 27:1; Rom. 2:1, 3, 12, 16, 27; 3:4, 6, 7; 14:3-5, 10, 13, 22; 1 Cor. 2:2; 4:5; 5:3, 12, 13; 6:2f., 6; 7:37; 10:15, 29; 11:13, 31, 32; 2 Cor. 2:1; 5:14; Col. 2:1, 16; 2 Thess. 2:12; 2 Tim. 4:1; Tit. 3:12; Heb. 10:30; 13:4; Jas. 2:12; 4:11f.; 1 Pet. 1:17; 2:23; 4:5f.; Rev. 6:10; 11:18; 16:5; 18:8, 20; 19:2, 11; 20:12f.

13. *Ṣaddîq* occurs in Gen. 6:9; 18:23-26; Deut. 4:8; 16:19; 25:1; Pss. 1:5; 7:9; 34:15, 19, 21; 37:12, 16f., 29; 58:10f.; 72:7; 112:4; 116:5; Prov. 11:8; Isa. 26:2; 45:21; 53:11; Ezek. 18:5; 33:12.

14. *Ṣedeq* occurs in Lev. 19:15, 36; Deut. 1:16; 16:18, 20; 25:15; Job 8:3; 31:6; Pss. 7:8, 17; 9:8; 18:20; 23:3; 65:5; 72:2; 85:10f.; 89:14; 119:75; Prov. 1:3; Isa. 42:6; Jer. 31:23; Ezek. 45:10; Hos. 2:19; Zeph. 2:3.

15. *Ṣedāqâ* occurs in Gen. 15:6; 18:19; Deut. 9:5; 24:13; 33:21; 2 Sam. 8:15; 19:28; Neh. 2:20; Pss. 31:1; 99:4; 106:31; 143:11; Isa. 9:7; 28:17; 32:17; Jer. 4:2; 9:24; 22:3, 15; Ezek. 14:14, 20; 18:5, 21.

16. *Dikaiosynē* occurs in Matt. 3:15; 5:6, 10, 20; 6:33; 21:32; Luke 1:75; John

uprightness, righteousness (whether of persons, motives, or actions); fulfilling divine statutes; righteousness bestowed by God," *dikaiōsis,*[17] "justification, vindication, acquittal," *dikaiōma,*[18] "regulation, requirement, commandment; righteous deed; justification (the last only in Rom. 5:16)," *dikē,*[19] "(just) penalty, punishment," and *dikaios,*[20] "(of people) upright, just, righteous (conforming to the laws of God); (of God in judging people and nations) just, righteous; (of things) right, righteous, innocent; what is obligatory in light of the standards of justice."

Hebrew *ṣādaq*[21] means "be just, righteous; have a just cause; be justified in a plea; be just or righteous in character or conduct; do justice by justifying someone or declaring someone righteous; save someone, vindicate someone's cause; make righteous, turn to righteousness." It corresponds closely to Greek *dikaioō,*[22] "show or do justice; justify, vindicate, or treat as just; be acquitted, be pronounced or treated as righteous, be justified; make free; be set free; be proved to be right," and *dikaiōs,*[23] "justly, in a just manner; uprightly."

16:8, 10; Acts 10:35; 13:10; 17:31; 24:25; Rom. 1:17; 3:5, 21f., 25f.; 4:3, 5f., 9, 11, 13, 22; 5:17, 21; 6:13, 16, 18-20; 8:10; 9:28, 30f.; 10:3-6, 10; 14:17; 1 Cor. 1:30; 2 Cor. 3:9; 5:21; 6:7, 14; 9:9f.; 11:15; Gal. 2:21; 3:6, 21; 5:5; Eph. 4:24; 5:9; 6:14; Phil. 1:11; 3:6, 9; 1 Tim. 6:11; 2 Tim. 2:22; 3:16; 4:8; Tit. 3:5; Heb. 1:9; 5:13; 7:2; 11:7, 33; 12:11; Jas. 1:20; 2:23; 3:18; 1 Pet. 2:24; 3:14; 2 Pet. 1:1; 2:5, 21; 3:13; 1 John 2:29; 3:7, 10; Rev. 19:11.

17. *Dikaiōsis* occurs in Rom. 4:25; 5:18.

18. *Dikaiōma* occurs in Luke 1:6; Rom. 1:32; 2:26; 5:16, 18; 8:4; Heb. 9:1, 10; Rev. 15:4; 19:8.

19. *Dikē* occurs in Acts 25:15; 28:4; 2 Thess. 1:9; Jude 1:7.

20. *Dikaios* occurs in Matt. 1:19; 5:45; 9:13; 10:41; 13:17, 43, 49; 20:4, 7; 23:28, 29, 35; 25:37, 46; 27:19, 24; Mark 2:17; 6:20; Luke 1:6f.; 2:25; 5:32; 12:57; 14:14; 15:7; 18:9; 20:20; 23:47, 50; John 3:14; 4:19; 7:24, 52; 10:22; 17:25; 22:14; 24:15; Acts 3:14; 4:19; 7:52; 10:22; 22:14; 24:15; Rom. 1:17; 2:13; 3:10, 26; 5:7, 19; 7:12; Gal. 3:11; Eph. 6:1; Phil. 1:7; 4:8; Col. 4:1; 2 Thess. 1:5f.; 1 Tim. 1:9; 2 Tim. 4:8; Tit. 1:8; Heb. 10:38; 11:4; 12:23; Jas. 5:6, 16; 1 Pet. 3:12, 18; 4:18; 2 Pet. 1:13; 2:7f.; 1 John 1:9; 2:1, 29; 3:7, 12; Rev. 15:3; 16:5, 7; 19:2; 22:11.

21. *Ṣādaq* occurs in Gen. 38:26; 44:16; Exod. 23:7; Deut. 25:1; 2 Sam. 15:4; 1 Kgs. 8:32; Job 4:17; 9:2, 20; 11:2; 33:12; Pss. 19:9; 51:4; 82:3; 143:2; Prov. 17:15; Isa. 5:23; 50:8; 43:9, 26; 53:11; Ezek. 16:51f.; Dan. 8:14; 12:3.

22. *Dikaioō* occurs in Matt. 11:19; 12:37; Luke 7:29, 35; 10:29; 16:15; 18:14; Acts 13:39; Rom. 2:13; 3:4, 20, 24, 26, 28, 30; 4:2, 5; 5:1, 9; 6:7; 8:30, 33; 1 Cor. 4:4; 6:11; Gal. 2:16f.; 3:8, 11, 24; 5:4; 1 Tim. 3:16; Tit. 3:7; Jas. 2:21, 24f.; Rev. 22:11.

23. *Dikaiōs* occurs in Luke 23:41; 1 Cor. 15:34; 1 Thess. 2:10; Tit. 2:12; 1 Pet. 2:23.

In the present discussion, it is important to note that none of these words has a meaning related to providing some benefit other than what is deserved. These words focus not on charity (grace) but on right and truth.

The First View Is Biblical

A comprehensive study of these words in the original languages and in their contexts supports the view of justice stated in the first sentence of paragraph 38 of the Declaration. In the drafting process, I was the primary author of what became that sentence. To make its implications explicit, let me revise it slightly: *The Biblical concept of justice may be summarized as rendering impartially to everyone his or her due in proper proportion according to the norm of God's moral law.* This definition reveals four main criteria of justice: *impartiality, rendering of what is due, proportionality,* and *normativity,* that is, conformity with a norm.

The first criterion of justice, *impartiality,* is fairness, a lack of bias or favoritism, an equal application of all relevant rules to all people in all relevant situations. When Moses commissioned the judges of Israel, he charged them:

> Give the members of your community a fair hearing, and judge rightly between one person and another, whether citizen or resident alien. You must not be partial in judging: hear out the small and the great alike; you shall not be intimidated by anyone, for the judgment is God's. (Deut. 1:16f.)

Here the key words are *šāpaṭ* ("give a hearing, judge"), *ṣedeq* ("rightly"), and *mišpāṭ* ("judgment"). Just judgment, then, is always *impartial* (cf. Exod. 23:3, 6; Lev. 19:15; Deut. 16:19; Job 13:10; Prov. 18:5; 24:23; 28:21; 1 Tim. 5:21; Jas. 2:1-9; 3:17). God is the chief exemplar of impartiality in judgment (Deut. 10:17; 2 Chr. 19:7; Job 13:8; Acts 10:34; Rom. 2:11; Eph. 6:9; Col. 3:25; 1 Pet. 1:17). God condemns all partiality in judgment or government (Ps. 82:2; Mal. 2:9).

The second criterion of justice is *rendering to each his or her due.* Paul instructs believers to "pay to all what is due to them" (Rom. 13:7), and he puts this instruction in a discussion of justice or judgment (in

v. 2 "judgment" is *krima*). Again, God is the chief exemplar: "Will he not repay all according to their deeds?" (Prov. 24:12; cf. Matt. 16:27; Rom. 2:6; 1 Cor. 3:8; Gal. 6:7f.); here "repay" translates a Hebrew verb meaning "turn back" or "return," whether physically, as from place to place, metaphorically, as in turning back to God, or retributively, as in making requital, whether justly (reward for good, punishment for wrong) or unjustly (returning evil for good or good for evil). Similarly, the Greek word translated "pay" in Rom. 13:7 means "reward" or "recompense."

Therefore, *a key concept in justice is that something about the recipient of an act (especially a judgment) merits or warrants the act (or judgment).* This is reinforced in Rom. 13:7 in the phrase "what is due to them." Sometimes what is due is determined by *who someone is,* for example, governing authorities (Rom. 13:1-7; 1 Pet. 2:13f.), parents (Eph. 6:1-3; Col. 3:20; Deut. 5:16), or religious leaders (Heb. 13:17; Acts 23:1-5). Sometimes, however, what is due is determined by *what someone does.* For example, elders are due *double* honor if they rule well (1 Tim. 5:17), the proud are due punishment (Ps. 94:2), murderers deserve death (Gen. 9:6), and so on. The case laws of Exodus 21 and 22 detail what is due to various crimes and torts against persons and property, all as matters of justice or judgment: "These are the judgments [*mišpāṭîm,* NRSV "ordinances"] that you shall set before them" (21:1).

The third criterion of justice, *proportionality,* entails *symmetry between rewards and punishments on the one hand and the acts in return for which they are rendered on the other.* This principle displays itself in Scripture in two ways. First, proportionality distinguishes generally between violations of property and violations of persons, prescribing different kinds and degrees of punishment for the two (Lev. 24:17-21). Second, proportionality distinguishes accidental harm, negligent harm, and intentional harm. For instance, if someone *accidentally* damages or destroys a neighbor's property, justice is served by evening up the loss between the two (Exod. 21:35). But if a person might reasonably have foreseen and prevented the accident but did not and so harms the neighbor *negligently,* then that person must bear the full loss alone, restoring to the neighbor the full value of what was damaged or destroyed (Exod. 21:36; cf. 22:6). And if a person *intentionally* steals or destroys a neighbor's property, then that person must restore what was taken plus some multiple of it as punishment for his or her wicked intent

(Exod. 22:1). Similarly, *accidental* homicide deserves no punishment, and the one who committed it must be protected from anyone who would try to wreak vengeance (Deut. 19:4-6; Exod. 21:13). But *negligent* homicide deserves death, though the heirs of the deceased (or possibly the judges) may permit a ransom (Exod. 21:29f.). And the *intentional* murderer must be executed without pity (Deut. 19:11-13; Exod. 21:14), no ransom being permitted (Num. 35:31). Corporal punishment short of execution also is to be proportionate to the magnitude of the offense (Deut. 25:1-3), as is all punishment or restitution (Exod. 21:24-27; Lev. 24:19f.). Even hell has degrees of torment proportionate to degrees of wickedness in this life (Luke 12:42-48).

The fourth criterion of justice, *normativity*, means that what is done is *according to a norm or standard;* it conforms with a rule. In this respect, *justice or righteousness is closely akin to truthfulness and honesty.* Thus, for instance, God commanded Israel, "You shall not cheat [RSV "do no wrong in judgment"] in measuring length, weight, or quantity. You shall have honest balances [literally "scales of *righteousness"*], honest weights, an honest ephah, and an honest hin" (Lev. 19:35f.): Measures of length, weight, and volume were to be just, that is, in accord with unchanging standards. This has direct application to economic relationships because it means that justice requires absolute honesty in all exchanges.

This application appears more clearly in Deut. 25:13-16 (cf. Job 31:6; Ezek. 45:10):

> You shall not have in your bag two kinds of weights, large and small. You shall not have in your house two kinds of measures, large and small. You shall have only a full and honest weight; you shall have only a full and honest measure, so that your days may be long in the land that the Lord your God is giving you. For all who do such things, all who act dishonestly, are abhorrent to the Lord your God.

By using differing weights (as counterweights in a balance scale) and measures, buyers and sellers could defraud each other by measuring more or less of something when it was to their benefit to do so, appearing to measure the same amount all the time. Apparently just such unjust trading practices were on God's mind in what is said through Micah, that God's people must "do justice" (Mic. 6:8), for God goes on to say to "the city":

Can I forget the treasures of wickedness in the house of the
wicked,
    and the scant measure that is accursed?
Can I tolerate wicked scales
    and a bag of dishonest weights?
Your wealthy are full of violence;
    your inhabitants speak lies,
    with tongues of deceit in their mouths. (Vv. 10-12)

Yet another means of deceitful injustice in trading was to dilute the
purity of goods (including gold or silver coin or bullion used as money)
offered in trade, a practice God condemns and uses as a metaphor for
the wickedness of rebellious hearts (Isa. 1:21-26; Ezek. 22:17-22).

Three Types of Relationships, Five Types of Justice

Justice governs all human relationships, but what it requires and permits
differs according to what relationships are involved. The table below
shows the three primary types of relationships, the five types of justice,
and what each type requires in the relationships to which it applies.

Voluntary Relationships	Involuntary Relationships	Accidental Relationships
Commutative Justice: Freewill exchange of value for value in trade among individuals	*Punitive Justice:* Visitation of punishment on one who violates another's rights	*Remedial Justice:* Restoration of persons to proportionately the same relationship they had before an accidental injury of one by another
Distributive Justice: Generalization (or distribution) of commutative justice systematically throughout a population by prohibiting, preventing, prosecuting, and punishing violations of commutative justice	*Vindicative Justice:* Acquittal of the innocent charged with a crime; restoration of victims by requiring those who harm them to pay restitution	

E. CALVIN BEISNER

Commutative and Distributive Justice

In voluntary exchanges, *commutative justice* is the principle that value must be exchanged for value without deception or coercion. The fundamental premise of commutative justice is the eighth commandment: "You shall not steal" (Exod. 20:15). All laws against theft, fraud, or cheating and laws requiring performance of contracts (oaths, vows, or promises) express this basic law. For instance: "You shall not steal; you shall not deal falsely; and you shall not lie to one another. . . . You shall not defraud your neighbor; you shall not steal; and you shall not keep for yourself the wages of a laborer until morning" (Lev. 19:11, 13). An implication of commutative justice is that if we desire what another has, we must offer something that that neighbor prefers in exchange for it, not acquire it by force or fraud. This message is implicit in Eph. 4:28: "Thieves must give up stealing; rather let them labor and work honestly with their own hands, so as to have something," and Paul turns from justice, which requires work rather than theft, to grace when he completes this exhortation with "something to share with the needy." Violations of commutative justice by fraud, theft, or violence bring punitive and vindicative justice (see below) into play as correctives.

Distributive justice should not be understood as determining the distribution of wealth or power in a population, as it often is, but as having to do with the distribution of justice itself: It is the universal application of rules without partiality or exception. Biblically rooted distributive justice, contrary to both moral relativism and utilitarianism (or consequentialism), insists that the same rules must apply to all people. Neither specific results nor consideration of who owns what, who has power, and the like, but just processes — impartiality, rendering what is due, proportionality, and conformity to the norm or standard — are required by distributive justice. Thus it is a hallmark of the Rule of Law that the concrete, historical results of particular laws or regulations in the lives of particular individuals or groups must be unpredictable, because the results must be conditioned on how people respond to laws, which varies from person to person, not on the laws alone. Laws requiring equal justice to all, regardless of their status in society, enunciate this principle.

Fundamental to distributive justice, then, is the distinction between formal laws and substantive rules. As Friedrich Hayek put it,

68

The difference between the two kinds of rules is the same as that between laying down a Rule of the Road, as in the Highway Code, and ordering people where to go; or, better still, between providing signposts and commanding people which road to take. . . . In fact, that we do *not* know their concrete effect, that we do *not* know what particular ends these rules will further, or which particular people they will assist, that they are merely given the form most likely on the whole to benefit all the people affected by them, is the most important criterion of formal rules in the sense in which we here use this term. . . .

A necessary, and only apparently paradoxical, result of this is that formal equality before the law is in conflict, and in fact incompatible, with any activity of the government deliberately aiming at material or substantive equality of different people, and that any policy aiming directly at a substantive ideal of distributive justice must lead to the destruction of the Rule of Law. To produce the same result for different people, it is necessary to treat them differently.[24]

What Hayek calls *formal* law or justice is what I mean by *distributive justice*. His term *substantive rule* is related to the idea of positive rights, that is, rights — not conditioned on the acts of the person having the rights — to the provision or acquisition of particular things (food, clothing, shelter, health care, education, etc.) rather than to just treatment. The principle of positive rights, because it ignores the conditionality entailed by the principle that justice requires rendering what is due, is inconsistent with distributive justice.[25]

Many people can readily obtain commutative justice for themselves, but *a general system of protection* (distributive justice) is necessary for those who, for various reasons, are especially vulnerable to injustice: "You shall not withhold the wages of [RSV "oppress"] poor and needy laborers, whether other Israelites or aliens who reside in your land in one of your towns" (Deut. 24:14; cf. Lev. 19:13; Deut. 15:7-18; Prov. 14:31; Amos 4:1; Mal. 3:5; 1 Tim. 5:18).

24. Friedrich A. Hayek, *The Road to Serfdom* (Chicago: University of Chicago, 1944), pp. 74f., 79. The whole of chapter 6, "Planning and the Rule of Law," is invaluable for understanding the meaning of distributive justice and the Rule of Law.

25. For a critique of positive rights, see Walter Block, "Private Property, Ethics, and Wealth Creation," in *The Capitalist Spirit: Toward a Religious Ethic of Capitalism*, ed. Peter L. Berger (San Francisco: Institute for Contemporary Studies, 1990).

You shall not wrong or oppress a resident alien, for you were aliens in the land of Egypt. You shall not abuse any widow or orphan. If you do abuse them, when they cry out to me, I will surely heed their cry; my wrath will burn, and I will kill you with the sword, and your wives shall become widows and your children orphans. (Exod. 22:21-24; cf. 23:9; Deut. 10:19; 24:17f.; Prov. 23:10f.; Jer. 7:6f.; Zech. 7:10; Jas. 1:27)

One should notice here the symmetry between the punishment God threatens and the offense. This illustrates the principle that justice renders to each what is due, as we have mentioned. We must not use the inability of some oppressed people to defend or vindicate themselves as an excuse to subvert the norms of justice.

Punitive and Vindicative Justice

When someone is forced to suffer a wrong, that person is oppressed, that is, treated with injustice, which is a violation of commutative or distributive justice. In response, God calls us to *vindicate* that person, to set things right.

Rectifying (vindicating) actions have two persons in view: the perpetrator of the injustice, and the victim. *Punitive justice* relates to the perpetrator and involves visiting on him or her the *due penalty* for the injustice. *Vindicative* and *retributive justice* relate to the victim and involve judging that person right in his or her complaint (vindicating him or her) and restoring to that person what was lost (procuring retribution [from Latin *re*, "back," and *tribuere*, "pay"] from the perpetrator).

In *crimes against property* (theft, destruction), punitive and retributive justice combine in the criminal's restoration to the victim of what was taken or destroyed (retribution or restitution) plus some additional amount (punishment). For instance, in theft,

- If the thief voluntarily confesses the crime and makes restitution, he or she is to repay what was stolen plus 20 percent (Lev. 5:14-16; 6:1-5; 22:14; Num. 5:5-8).
- If the thief is caught, he or she is to repay what what was stolen plus the same value again. That is, restitution is double (Exod. 22:4, 7).

- In certain instances and for reasons difficult to determine today, when the thief steals livestock and slaughters or sells it, restitution is fourfold for a sheep or fivefold for an ox (Exod. 22:1).
- If a starving person steals food and is caught, restitution must be "sevenfold" (Prov. 6:30f.), an idiomatic expression meaning that the full restitution prescribed by the law — whatever the multiple — must be paid and that the thief's crisis excuses neither the crime nor the imposition of a lesser penalty by a judge.

In *crimes against persons,* punitive justice requires the suffering of some loss by the criminal, and retributive (vindicative) justice requires the criminal to bear the costs of the injury — except in murder, in which case the criminal is to bear the same loss as the victim — death (see Exod. 21:12-27). It is important to note that the Bible considers false accusation of a crime to be a crime itself. Vindicative justice is done when one falsely accused is declared innocent and the accuser is made to suffer the penalty associated with the alleged crime (Deut. 19:16-19).

Remedial Justice

Sometimes people damage others' property by pure accident, meaning that neither ill intent nor negligence is involved. In such cases, biblical justice requires the one who causes the loss to share the cost equally with the victim (Exod. 21:35). But if negligence is involved (meaning the harm is not purely accidental), the negligent person must bear the whole loss (vv. 33f., 36). Or if the property is rented, accidental damage of it is considered to be covered by the rent (22:15b), unless a prior agreement specifies that accidental damage during the renter's possession requires additional payment.

In its punitive, vindicatory, and remedial senses, justice often comes to the special aid of the poor.

Justice and the Poor

Scripture forbids partiality either in favor of or against the poor (Exod. 23:3, 6; Lev. 19:15). Nonetheless, the Old Testament also frequently

71

associates help for the poor with justice (Pss. 72:2, 4; 82:3; 140:12; Prov. 29:14; 31:9). Why?

It does so because the poor are particularly vulnerable to injustice in ways others are not and are therefore victims of injustice more frequently than most others. Furthermore, often the many Hebrew words translated "poor" in these contexts emphasize not the material destitution of those involved but their weakness, dependence, or low status in society and hence the likelihood that they will be oppressed.[26] In other words, it is not simply because such people are materially lacking that Scripture tells us to help them by administering justice on their behalf, that is, by justifying or vindicating them, but because they are victims of injustice (e.g., Pss. 72:4; 74:21; 82:3; 109:31; 140:12; Prov. 22:22; 28:3; Eccl. 5:8; Isa. 3:14; 10:2; 11:4; Jer. 5:28; Amos 2:6; 5:12). In contrast, we are to exercise charity, or grace, toward them simply because they are materially lacking, whether they deserve help or not (Deut. 15:7-11; Ps. 112:9; Prov. 19:17; 22:9; 28:27; Matt. 19:21; Mark 10:21; Luke 19:8; 2 Cor. 9:6-9).

Consequently, the Old Testament frequently speaks of the poor in much the same way that it speaks of other vulnerable people, for example, widows, orphans, and strangers (see Deut. 10:18). For instance, a prayer regarding the ideal king (ultimately the Messiah) is:

> May he judge your [God's] people with righteousness,
> and your poor with justice. . . .
> May he defend the cause of the poor of the people,
> give deliverance to the needy,
> and crush the oppressor. (Ps. 72:2, 4)[27]

---

26. Additional discussion of the meaning and usage of the biblical vocabulary of the poor is beyond the scope of this article, but it is crucial to the understanding of the application of justice to the poor. A very helpful study of the former is Daryl S. Borgquist, *Toward a Biblical Theology of the Poor* (Master of Theological Studies thesis, Talbot Theological Seminary, 1983).

27. Here "judge" is Hebrew *dyn,* that is, "plead the cause; execute judgment, vindicate, requite; govern"; "righteousness" is *ṣedeq;* the "poor" are the *ʿanîm,* that is, those who are "needy, weak, afflicted, humble," but not necessarily materially lacking; "justice" is *mišpāṭ;* the king's defense of the cause of the poor is expressed with *šāpaṭ;* the "needy" are the *ʾebyônîm,* those who are "in want or materially lacking"; and the oppressor is the *ʿāšaq,* i.e., one who deals deceitfully, defrauds, oppresses, or does violence.

So frequently are the *materially poor* also the *oppressed or afflicted* that the two Hebrew words denoting these are sometimes used interchangeably, as here in Ps. 72 (the "needy" and the "poor") and in the parallelism of Ps. 74:21: "Do not let the downtrodden [i.e., "oppressed"] be put to shame; let the poor and needy praise your name." Here the "oppressed" simply *are* those in need. The same idea occurs in Ps. 82:3: "Give justice to [*šāpaṭ*, "judge, vindicate"] the weak [*dal*, low, thin, reduced, helpless] and the orphan; maintain the right [*ṣādaq*] of the lowly [*ʿānî*] and the destitute [*rāš*, "in want, lacking, poor"]." While justice, then, is never *partial* to the poor (Exod. 23:3), it recognizes that the poor are often vulnerable to injustice and so is particularly apt to come to their aid in vindication, justification, or salvation from those who oppress them (see also Ps. 140:12; Prov. 29:7, 14; 31:9; Eccl. 5:8; Isa. 3:14; 10:2; 11:4; 32:7; Jer. 5:28; 22:16; Ezek. 18:17; Amos 5:12).

The key point is that when the Bible speaks of doing *justice* for or to the poor, it speaks in light of their having suffered *injustice*. When, in contrast, it speaks of helping the poor simply because they are poor, not because they are oppressed, it speaks in terms of charity or grace.

The Second View Is Unbiblical

The second view of justice in the Oxford Declaration obscures the distinction between justice, on the one hand, and grace (or charity) and love, on the other. This leads to serious misconceptions of both biblical ethics and the theology of salvation.

The confusion is most apparent in the assertion that Paul used *justice* as "a metaphor to describe God's creative and powerful redemptive love." The Declaration cites Rom. 1:17f.; 3:21-26 and Eph. 2:4-22 as examples of this usage. A careful examination of these passages, however, indicates that they exemplify nothing of the sort.

In Rom. 1:16-18, Paul writes,

> I am not ashamed of the gospel; it is the power of God for salvation to everyone who has faith, to the Jew first and also to the Greek. For in it the righteousness [*dikaiosynē*] of God is revealed through faith for faith; as it is written, "The one who is righteous [*dikaios*] will live by faith."

73

For the wrath of God is revealed from heaven against all ungod-
liness and wickedness [*adikia,* i.e., "unrighteousness"] of those who
by their wickedness suppress the truth.

Aside from the fact that *justice* or *righteousness* is not used metaphorically in this passage, the righteousness of God of which Paul here writes
is a righteousness given by God to believers as the ground of their
justification. Apart from this *gift* of righteousness, they, like all people,
would be unrighteous and so subject to God's wrath (v. 18). Verse 17,
then, functions as an explication of verse 16, as Calvin pointed out:

> This is an explanation and a confirmation of the preceding clause,
> which stated that the Gospel is "the power of God unto salvation."
> If we seek salvation, i.e. life with God, we must first seek righteous-
> ness, by which we may be reconciled to Him, and obtain that life
> which consists in His benevolence alone through His being favour-
> able to us. In order that we may be loved by God we must first be
> righteous, for He hates unrighteousness. The meaning is, therefore,
> that we can obtain salvation from no other source than the Gospel,
> since God has nowhere else revealed to us His righteousness, which
> alone delivers us from death. This righteousness, the basis of our
> salvation, is revealed in the Gospel: hence the Gospel is said to be
> *the power of God unto salvation.* In this way we argue from cause
> to effect.
>
> Note further how rare and valuable a treasure God bestows on us
> in His Gospel, viz. *the communication of His righteousness.*[28]

This righteousness "cannot here be understood of a divine attribute,"
writes Charles Hodge, ". . . because it is . . . *a righteousness which is
by faith, i.e.,* attained by faith, of which the apostle speaks. Besides, it
is elsewhere said to be without law [Rom. 3:21], to be a gift [5:17], not
to be our own [10:3], to be from God [Phil. 3:9]."[29] Put simply, verse 17

28. John Calvin, *The Epistles of Paul the Apostle to the Romans and to the
Thessalonians,* tr. Ross MacKenzie (Grand Rapids: Eerdmans, 1960), pp. 27f., emphasis
in second paragraph added.

29. Charles Hodge, *Commentary on the Epistle to the Romans* (rev. ed., 1886;
reprint, Grand Rapids: Eerdmans, 1977), p. 30. For other arguments to the same conclusion, see David Brown, *The Epistle of Paul the Apostle to the Romans,* in Robert
Jamieson, A. R. Fausset, and David Brown, *A Commentary, Critical, Experimental,*

explains how the gospel mentioned in verse 16 can be "the power of God for salvation to everyone who has faith." It can be because the good news of the gospel is that God's righteousness is given by God to those who believe, who without that gift of righteousness (Rom. 5:17) would be unrighteous and therefore would suffer divine wrath (1:18).

In Rom. 3:21-26, Paul writes,

> But now, apart from law, the righteousness *[dikaiosynē]* of God has been disclosed, and is attested by the law and the prophets, the righteousness of God through faith in Jesus Christ for all who believe. For there is no distinction, since all have sinned and fall short of the glory of God; they are now justified *[dikaioumenoi]* by his grace as a gift, through the redemption that is in Christ Jesus, whom God put forward as a sacrifice of atonement by his blood, effective through faith. He did this to show his righteousness, because in his divine forbearance he had passed over the sins previously committed; it was to prove at the present time that he himself is righteous and that he justifies the one who has faith in Jesus.

Here again, "righteousness/justice" is not used metaphorically, and it clearly is not the inherent righteousness or justice of God that Paul has in mind when he writes of "the righteousness of God" disclosed "apart from the law" that is "through faith in Jesus Christ for all who believe." Rather it is the gift of righteousness (Rom. 5:17) received "through faith" and given to all who believe.

Righteousness as God's character does, indeed, come into view in verses 25f., but not as the motive or ground of God's saving sinners through justification, but as the attribute of God that might have been questioned were it not for the *gift* of righteousness granted to believers.

---

and Practical on the Old and New Testaments (reprint, Grand Rapids: Eerdmans, 1976, reprint) III/2, p. 195; Robert Haldane, *An Exposition of Romans* (reprint, McLean, VA: MacDonald, 1958), pp. 48f.; R. C. H. Lenski, *The Interpretation of St. Paul's Epistle to the Romans* (1936; reprint, Minneapolis: Augsburg, 1961), pp. 78-80; Martin Luther, *Lectures on Romans,* tr. and ed. Wilhelm Pauck (Philadelphia: Westminster, 1961), p. 18; H. C. G. Moule, *Studies in Romans* (1892; reprint, Grand Rapids: Kregel, 1977), p. 57; John Murray, *The Epistle to the Romans* (Grand Rapids: Eerdmans, 1980), pp. 30f. Luther (loc. cit.) cites Augustine, *On the Spirit and the Letter:* "The righteousness of God is that righteousness which he imparts in order to make men righteous. Just as that is the Lord's salvation by which he saves us."

God would have been unjust to give a simple declaration that those who had no righteousness were now righteous (justified); but the gospel tells us that there is a righteousness given by God, the righteousness of Jesus Christ, that merits the declaration of righteousness for the believer (cf. Rom. 5:15-19). This is the same righteousness of which Paul elsewhere writes:

> I regard everything as loss because of the surpassing value of knowing Christ Jesus my Lord. For his sake I have suffered the loss of all things, and I regard them as rubbish, in order that I may gain Christ and be found in him, *not having a righteousness of my own that comes from the law, but one that comes through faith in Christ, the righteousness from God based on faith.* (Phil. 3:8f.)

In Eph. 2:4-22, Paul never uses the words for righteousness or justice. Instead, he writes that

> God, who is rich in *mercy,* out of the great *love* with which he loved us even when we were dead through our trespasses, made us alive together with Christ — by *grace* you have been saved — and raised us up with him and seated us with him in the heavenly places in Christ Jesus, so that in the ages to come he might show *the immeasurable riches of his grace in kindness toward us in Christ Jesus.* For by *grace* you have been saved through faith, and this is not your own doing; it is the *gift* of God — not the result of works, so that no one may boast. (Vv. 4-9)

It is not God's justice but God's grace that is the motive cause for saving sinners, and Rom. 3:21-26 tells us that the gift of righteousness is the meritorious cause of that salvation, the cause that satisfies the demands of divine justice for righteousness in all who will come near to God.

Paul makes the distinction clear: Human righteousness (or justice) is "from the law" (Phil. 3:9). Therefore, since all have broken the law, no one is truly righteous in himself or herself (Rom. 3:9-20). If our justification were by the works of the law, it would not be "reckoned as a gift [*charis,* i.e., "grace"] but as something due" (Rom. 4:4; cf. 3:20–4:3). Paul's choice of words is significant here in light of later usage. Here he argues that whatever is of grace cannot be of debt (*opheilēma*). But later, when he tells us that justice requires that we

76

render to everyone his *due* (*opheilas;* Rom. 13:7), he uses the same root. We may infer, then, that whatever is of justice is not of grace, and whatever is of grace is not of justice.

This is why it is so dangerous to confuse justice and grace, as occurs in the second view of justice in the Declaration. To say, "Paul uses justice . . . as a metaphor to describe God's . . . redemptive love," and then to attribute redemption to grace (38, third sentence), is to imply that God's saving sinners was not a gracious gift of God's righteousness to them but an act of divine justice toward them. It is to imply that somehow sinners were *due* redemption, not that it was granted us as an unmerited gift.

The ultimate danger of this confusion appears strongly in the Composite Discussion Document, paragraph 70, quoted in note 2 above. If, in the words of the document, "by God's grace what is due to us . . . is to . . . belong to God," then the logical implication is that everyone is due redemption, everyone is due salvation. But Paul's words answer directly: "Now to one who *works*, wages are not reckoned as a gift [*charis*, i.e., grace] but as something due" (Rom. 4:4) and "by *grace* you have been saved through faith, and this is not your own doing; it is the gift of God — *not the result of works*, so that no one may boast" (Eph. 2:8f.). Belonging to God is *due* to no one; it is given freely to those who deserve the opposite (Rom. 6:23). If, as the Composite Discussion Document says, "what love desires, justice demands," then is everyone *due* whatever someone who *loves* that person desires him or her to have? What if the one who loves cannot provide the thing desired? Whose duty is it to provide it? Who will be charged with injustice if it is never provided? Confusing love or grace with justice leads inexorably to such insoluble conundrums.

Furthermore, although all of God's attributes are internally consistent, they have different effects outwardly on God's creatures. As we have seen, the effect of God's grace toward sinners contrasts with that of God's justice. From God's justice flows the condemnation of the unrighteous, that is, of *all*, "since all have sinned and fall short of the glory of God." From God's grace flows the justification of some of the unrighteous, namely, those who are made righteous, those to whom God gives the gift of righteousness so that God "prove . . . that he himself is righteous and that he justifies the one who has faith in Jesus" (Rom. 3:26).

And this is precisely why *grace exceeds justice as a remedy of the troubles of the poor.* Although some of the troubles of the poor are caused by injustice, others are justly deserved, for the poor are not exempt from sin just because they are poor. Indeed, that any sinner

77

enjoys any benefit is a sign of God's grace to that person, since all deserve nothing but God's wrath (Rom. 1:18). Doing justice for the poor, then, might relieve them of some of their troubles; it might even go a long way toward ameliorating their circumstances. But just as lost sinners need not just judgment but gracious pardon from God ("Blessed are those whose iniquities are forgiven, and whose sins are covered; blessed is the one against whom the Lord will not reckon sin," Rom. 4:7f.), so the poor need, as a remedy for their own failings, not justice but charity (*charis,* grace).

It is troubling, therefore, to see some writers disparage charity in contrast with justice when discussing the needs of the poor. For instance, Ronald Sider writes of the sabbatical year debt relief: "It is crucial to note that Scripture prescribes justice rather than *mere* charity."[30] *Mere* charity? *Mere* grace? Does this sound like Paul's exultations that God "destined us for adoption as his children through Jesus Christ, according to the good pleasure of his will, *to the praise of his glorious grace*" (Eph. 1:5f.) or that "we have redemption through his blood, the forgiveness of our tresspasses, according to *the riches of his grace*" (v. 7) or that "God, who is rich in mercy, out of the great love with which he loved us even when we were dead through our trespasses, made us alive together in Christ — by grace you have been saved — and raised us up with him and seated us with him in the heavenly places in Christ Jesus, *so that in the ages to come he might show* THE IMMEASURABLE RICHES OF HIS GRACE IN KINDNESS *TOWARD US IN CHRIST JESUS*" (Eph. 2:4-7)?

Properly understood, charity — that is, grace — should never be thought a less appropriate response to people's needs than justice. Where the needy suffer because they have been unjustly treated, they need justice and, if that is not attainable, charity. Where they suffer because they have harmed themselves, or by historical circumstances (really, divine providence), they need charity. Paul's high view of grace cannot be reconciled with a disparaging view of charity to the poor. The same glorious grace that, in God, motivated the atonement should, in us, underlie our understanding of economic charity and motivate our exercise of it. By drawing this connection between the grace of atonement and the grace of economic charity we do not demean the former but

---

30. Ronald J. Sider, *Rich Christians in an Age of Hunger: A Biblical Study,* 2d ed. (Downers Grove: InterVarsity, 1984), p. 83; 3d ed. (Waco: Word, 1990), p. 68, emphasis added. See also 3d ed., p. 71: "God wills justice, not mere charity."

elevate the latter (charity) by associating the two, just as Paul does when he makes the grace of Christ in atonement the paradigm for the grace of the Corinthians in giving to the needy saints of Jerusalem: "For you know the generous act [*charis*] of our Lord Jesus Christ, that though he was rich, yet for your sakes he became poor, so that by his poverty you might become rich" (2 Cor. 8:9).

Let there be no misunderstanding. Refusing to equate justice with grace or love does not mean denying the necessity of obedience to God's commands by those who profess faith in Christ Jesus, and *God's commands include the command to exercise grace to the poor.* Practical righteousness or justice, therefore, requires *graciously* serving the poor — and not only the poor but all people with all kinds of needs. Believers, individually and corporately, owe God this gracious service to the needy as a matter of obedience. use

But if the benefits of the gracious service to the needy that God commands are made a matter of our justice *to the needy* rather than of our justice *to God,* then grace becomes law, and law never saves. Then the needy — and those who merely profess to be needy — may claim the benefits of grace as their due by justice, appealing to the state for their enforcement, since God has ordained the state to enforce justice. That way lies the socialist welfare state — the enforcement of "charitable" aid by the coercive power of the state. Not only does biblical ethics, as I have argued above, stand against such a view of justice and the state, but history also tells us that the socialist welfare state succeeds only in multiplying the poor and their needs, not in lifting them out of poverty — a fact to which the Oxford Declaration, reinforced by Pope John Paul II's *Centesimus Annus,* gives ample testimony.[31]

31. John Paul II, *Centesimus Annus,* May 1, 1991 (Washington: United States Catholic Conference, 1991), p. 61. For detailed arguments regarding the counterproductive (and unintended) consequences of the welfare state, see E. Calvin Beisner, *Prosperity and Poverty: The Compassionate Use of Resources in a World of Scarcity* (Westchester, IL: Crossway, 1988), pp. 183-87; Clarence Carson, *The War on the Poor* (New Rochelle, NY: Arlington, 1969); and Charles Murray, *Losing Ground: American Social Policy 1950-1980* (New York: Basic, 1984). The Oxford Declaration and *Centesimus Annus* address the historical failure of socialism chiefly in what are now formerly communist countries. The three books just listed address the failure of the welfare state to help the poor in democratic capitalist countries.

The proper alternative, however, is not the opposite extreme, individualism. Both extremes of the dialectic are contrary to Scripture. The proper alternative is obedience to the commands of God. When God commands justice, we do justice; when God commands grace, we exercise grace. When God ordains the state to enforce justice, not charity, the state must stay within its God-given boundaries. In the same way, when God commands private persons, both individually and corporately, to exercise charity, not (punitive) justice (Rom. 12:19), they must stay within their God-given boundaries. For the state to overstep its bounds and become a vigilante for charity is as wrong as for private persons to overstep their bounds and become vigilantes for (punitive) justice; the one leads ultimately to totalitarian socialism, the other to mob law. My quarrel is *not* with real caretaking but with an all-too-human methodology that must fail to serve the poor.

Indeed, the poor do need justice; *everyone* needs justice from fellow humans. It is the solemn obligation of everyone to do justice to everyone else, and particularly of governing authorities to enforce justice throughout the community (Rom. 13:1-4). But just as sinners need grace, so the poor need charity.

The Partiality of Biblical Justice: A Response to Calvin Beisner

Stephen Charles Mott

The well-known statue of the Greek goddess of justice portrays a woman with a blindfold over her eyes. Justice is to be carried out without seeing particular people. It is to be carried out without giving special personal favors. It is to be rendered with impartiality. Biblical justice may seem to be contrary to the very nature of justice with its partiality to the poor and disadvantaged. Biblical justice is especially difficult to understand for those who have grown up in a liberal culture. The liberal conception of justice stresses that everyone is to be treated in the same way.

A conception of justice corresponds to an understanding of the relationship that the individual has to society. The liberal view presupposes that individuals naturally live in separation from one another. Justice comes to play only to prevent their exercise of freedom from causing harm to one another. The biblical view, in contrast, assumes that people are social beings. Justice serves to enforce positive responsibilities of care for one another. In each case the government has the role of enforcing that which is regarded as of basic importance in social relationships.

The biblical sense of partiality in justice, however, is not a weird view, one that is contrary to reason or general human experience. Its insistence on special treatment of the poor in justice and law was shared throughout the ancient Near East. Even in western Mediterranean cultures, which stressed to a greater degree reciprocity among citizens, to the point of neglecting the mass of slaves, the emperor as the head of the community had a special concern for the welfare of the weak — the elderly, women, and children.[1] Most people would not have considered a society just if it treated a blind person, for instance, no differently from anyone else.

Liberalism has sought to deal with people abstractly as human beings. Basic decisions are to be made in terms of laws rather than of persons. The weakness of this approach has been the unusual difficulty it poses to giving recognition in justice to special needs. Its great strength, however, has been in challenging elitist privilege and providing civil rights impartially for everyone, as in the American Bill of Rights. Liberalism's success makes it proper that partialities that are to remain in justice be defended. How does recognition of special needs relate to the impartial character of justice?

This question is crucial for the direction of politics. If justice by its impartiality cannot take into consideration some people's lack of basic benefits of life in society, such as food, shelter, work, and health, then the role of the government on behalf of the needy would be rightly vastly restricted. It would justly do little beyond preventing the strong from taking advantage of the weak in acts that are intrinsically antisocial and wrong, such as robbery, fraud, or physical violence. To recognize a right to food, for example, forces the government to be partial. The task of government is defined by rights. Establishing a right to food would mean helping those who lack it to obtain it at a cost to other parts of society. Such a welfare role of the government has been denounced in the name of impartiality. Such legislation has been considered unjust because it "maintains the interest of one section of the populace against those of another."[2]

The Impartiality of Justice

The equality present in the impartiality that is to characterize justice does not mean that in justice all people are treated alike in all respects. It means that one does not *arbitrarily* treat one person less well than another.[3] A

1. Thomas Wiedemann, *Adults and Children in the Roman Empire* (New Haven: Yale University, 1989), p. 39.
2. Carl F. H. Henry, *Aspects of Christian Social Ethics* (Grand Rapids: Eerdmans, 1964), p. 155.
3. Edward V. Vacek, "Love of God, Love of Neighbor and Self" (unpublished, September 1991).

theory of justice provides criteria to indicate the grounds for just discrimination. *Impartiality* means that justice must treat all people alike in terms of these criteria. A particular individual is to receive no more than what is his or her due according to that theory of justice.

Justice in this way shows how we are to make choices in our love. *Love* is the impartial category. We are to love everyone as we love our own selves. Justice informs us how to make choices between neighbors when they present to us conflicting claims of love.[4] Justice demonstrates the meaning of love in frequent situations of social life.

Distributive justice, which is particularly at stake in this argument, provides the standard for how the advantages of life in society are to be distributed. This is the established use of the term. This use sets it in contrast to retributive or criminal justice. If one wished to use this particular term, *distributive justice,* for another function of justice, such as the fairness present in regulations of exchange and contract, one still needs to identify the standard accepted for the social function of distributing the benefits of life in society. All cultures have this function of justice, whether it is made explicit or not. If a culture or theory makes no special provision for distributive justice, then the standard becomes that of ability and might, modified only by voluntary actions. Such voluntary actions are insufficient in light of the biblical theory of justice and its realistic understanding of human nature. It is not surprising that the voluntaristic approach has an association with liberalism, with its shallow perspective on the depth of human self-interest and its failure to deal adequately with power and conflict.

All theories of distributive justice are partial according to the standard they provide. Ancient Greek justice, despite its blindfolded goddess, was partial. The citizen had just claims that slaves did not have. The criterion of distribution was in accordance with the alleged worth of one's contribution to society. Citizens received more because they were viewed as making greater contributions than did slaves.[5] Some social similarities and dissimilarities were thus recognized as necessary considerations for justice. Arbitrary behavior, or partiality, favored a particular individual beyond the limits of what was due according to this arrangement of society.

4. Lewis B. Smedes, "The Evangelicals and the Social Question," *Reformed Journal* 16, no. 2 (February 1966): 12.

5. Cf. Aristotle, *Politica* 1259b20-21; 1281a4-8; *Nicomachean Ethics* 1134a7-8; Plato, *Republic* 558c, 563.

Other theories may be partial to those of high birth or wealth. Liberal theory is partial to those who are able to prevail in the market. Such people are viewed as properly receiving more of society's material goods. Commutative justice leans toward those who are able to secure favorable arrangements in contracts and exchange.

Biblical justice is not distinctive by being impartial or by being partial. All theories of justice are both. Biblical justice has the premise that impartial treatment of all members of the community requires special attention to the groups in society that are most needy. Within the limits of what is due to the poor, it is partial to the poor.

Deut. 10:17 brings both of these elements together. In this statement of God's justice, it asserts that God "is not partial and takes no bribe." The passage immediately goes on to describe God as one "who executes justice for the orphan and the widow, and who loves the strangers, providing them food and clothing" (v. 18). These groups are singled out favorably in relationship to justice, in this passage as continually in the Bible.

This important passage, which summarizes God's requirements in response to the deliverance from Egypt, refuses to impose on the Old Testament separate spheres of love, which pertains to voluntary charity, and justice, which pertains to law. Similarly unfounded is the separation of justice from response to needs of the poor that are not the result of violations of fair processes. Justice is parallel with love here, and the benefits of food and clothing are given. What the groups named in this passage have in common is their need. It is not said that they are in need only as victims of explicit antisocial acts, such as fraud or robbery. The Bible in its impartiality is comfortable with its partial concern in justice for providing for those lacking in basic needs. The compartmentalizations of liberal culture are not supported by this text. They also are not supported by Hebrew culture in general nor ancient Near Eastern legal systems similar to that of ancient Israel.[6]

Similarly, Lev. 19:15 in discussing justice forbids giving favor to the poor or the great. It is immediately preceded, nevertheless, by injunctions that provide special protection only for groups of the needy. One is not to harvest completely one's own field or vineyards, but should leave food behind for the poor and the resident foreigners (vv. 9f.). The cause of their

---

6. See, e.g., J. P. J. Olivier, "The Sceptre of Justice and Ps. 45:7b," *Journal of Northwest Semitic Languages* 7 (1979): 50-52.

need is not mentioned. Further, the deaf are not to be ridiculed, nor are the blind in their weakness to be taken advantage of (v. 14). The wages of laborers are to be paid on the very day of their work (v. 13). Such a requirement might be a disadvantage or even hardship to the employer, who might otherwise contract more favorable arrangements. Payment not delayed indefinitely might seem fair enough, but the laborer's wage was his or her daily livelihood. Basic needs were at stake.

Biblical statements about not being partial to the poor thus in context do not exclude from the central concerns of justice the basic needs of the poor. Impartiality in justice merely means that in terms of justice the poor were not to be granted more than their just claims. This limitation was particularly important in judicial conflicts between members of the community. The poor did, however, have specific claims as members of a needy group. There was a *"mišpāṭ* of the needy" (Jer. 5:28; cf. Prov. 29:7) — just claims that belonged to the poor. A poor person had valid claims under God on the community, claims that were only present when a person was in need. Any member of the community, however, in becoming needy could make such a claim.

The formal equality of all before the law is particularly marked in *retributive justice* (the assigning of penalties for violating the standards of the community). Those who have broken the covenant and its standards are to bear the prescribed penalty no matter what their social standing. The dominant concern in these texts is on the power of wealth to corrupt the formal equality of the courts. In the instructions the focus is frequently on bribes.[7]

In passage after passage the groups to whom justice is to be applied are those whose basic needs are most at risk — the widow, the orphan, the resident alien, and the poor. If instead of these groups, the appeal continually made was for justice for the wealthy, landholders, nobles, and the mighty, one would correctly speak of a bias to the holders of power. There is a bias, but it is rather to the powerless.

The bias toward the weak, which is the most striking characteristic of biblical justice, does not mean that God loves the poor more or that they should receive more than their just claims. The poor are given priority

---

7. Exod. 18:21; 23:8; Deut. 16:18f.; 2 Chr. 19:7. Christopher J. H. Wright, particularly on the basis of Exod. 23:1-8, notes the special attention given to partiality toward witnesses in legal proceedings. *An Eye for an Eye: The Place of Old Testament Ethics Today* (Downers Grove: InterVarsity, 1983), pp. 170f.

only because their wretchedness requires greater attention if the equal regard called forth by the equal merit of all persons in the community is to be achieved. Justice must vindicate those who cannot themselves secure their own rights. This is the "deepseated and fundamental bias" at the root of prophetic understanding of justice.[8] In the concern for the basic needs of all, the equal provision of basic rights requires unequal response to unequal needs. Justice must be partial in order to be impartial.

In the raging social struggles in which the poor are perennially victims of injustice and denied basic needs, God takes up the cause of the weak, and thus the followers of God do as well. Throughout the Bible, rulers and leaders, within the theocracy and outside it, are to exercise justice by supporting the just claims of the weak and power-less.[9] Indeed, it is a standard of conduct for all of God's people. The images of justice involve interfering with oppressive behavior, avoiding actions that threaten the dignity and livelihood of the weak, and providing for their basic needs.[10]

Preference for the Poor

The Model of God's Justice

God's justice was the model of justice oriented to the needy.

> All my bones shall say,
>   "O Lord, who is like you?
> You deliver the weak
>   from those too strong for them,
> the weak and needy from those who despoil them." (Ps. 35:10)

The Lord, the mighty creator, is the one "who executes justice for the oppressed; who gives food to the hungry" (Ps. 146:7). This justice

---

8. Cf. Norman H. Snaith, *The Distinctive Ideas of the Old Testament* (London: Epworth, 1944), pp. 68, 71f.

9. Prov. 31:8f.; Ps. 72:1-4; Jer. 22:3, 14f.; Dan. 4:27; Matt. 23:23; cf. John W. Olley, " 'Righteousness' — Some Issues in Old Testament Translation into English," *Bible Translator* 38 (1987): 309, 314.

10. Job 29:14-17; Ezek. 18:5, 7; Deut. 24:10-17; Ps. 112:9; Amos 5:7, 11-15.

reaches out to the prisoners, the blind, those who are bowed down, the stranger, the orphan, and the widow (Ps. 146:9).

Justice is grounded in God's character as the sovereign creator of the universe (Ps. 99:1-4). God establishes justice for all the oppressed of the earth (Ps. 76:9; "earth" here is the inhabited world, in contrast to the heavens [v. 8; cf. v. 12]), not merely the land of Israel. Therefore justice exists before its expression in any particular covenant or dispensation. There are universal distributive concerns grounded in God's justice that are prior to the rules of exchange and contract. These Old Testament materials are normative for us today.

The justice that characterizes God's defense of the poor is the same justice that is demanded of humanity. In the Mosaic legislation the special care given to the socially and economically weak was based on God being a God of justice. It is "the LORD" "who executes justice (*mišpāṭ*) for the orphan and the widow, and who loves the strangers, providing them food and clothing. You shall also love the stranger . . ." (Deut. 10:18f.). It is methodologically necessary for us to look at the biblical materials describing God's social justice to develop the understanding of human responsibilities in justice.

Deliverance

Justice is rectification of the gross social inequities of the disadvantaged. It is not a mere *mitigation* of suffering in oppression. Justice is *deliverance*. In the midst of oppression God takes sides and brings the oppressed to security and well-being. The terms for justice are frequently associated with *yᵉšûʿâ*, the most important Hebrew word for deliverance and salvation: "God rose up to establish justice [*mišpāṭ*, NRSV "judgment"], to *save* [*hôšîaʿ*] all the oppressed of the earth" (Ps. 76:9; cf. Isa. 63:1).[11] "Give justice to the weak" and "maintain the right of the lowly" are parallel to "rescue the weak and the needy; deliver them from the hand of the wicked" (Ps. 82:3f.)[12]

Justice involves the deliverance of people from political and

---

11. Cf. also Pss. 40:10; 43:1f.; 71:1f., 24; 72:1-4; 116:5f.; Isa. 46:12f.; 59:11, 17; 45:8; 61:10; 62:1f.; 63:7f. LXX; 65:6; 119:123 and many other passages. With *pilleṭ* for "deliver" in Pss. 31:1; 37:28, 40.

12. Cf. Job 29:12, 14; Prov. 24:11.

economic oppressors (Judg. 5:11), from slavery (1 Sam. 12:7; Mic. 6:5), and from captivity (Isa. 41:1-11 [cf. *ṣedeq* in v. 2]; Jer. 51:10). Providing for the needy means setting them back on their feet, giving them a home, leading them to prosperity and restoration, and ending their oppression (Pss. 68:5-10; 10:15-18).[13] Justice removes oppression; it does not merely help the victims of oppression to cope within oppression.

The same combination of justice and deliverance from the power of the oppressor is demanded of the ruler (Jer. 21:12; 22:2f.; Ps. 72:4).[14] Justice in the Bible is an intervening power. God seeks those who will "repair the wall and stand in the breach before [God] in the land" (Ezek. 22:30) over against the oppression of the poor and weak (v. 29; cf. Isa. 59:15f.).

Restoration to Community

In the Bible we continually have before us justice as the correction of the situation in which the strong have exploitive power over the weak. In deliverance the people are returned to the situation of life in community that God intends for them. Justice is a restoration to community. As seen in the Jubilee provisions and as formulated in Lev. 25:35f., the poor are described as being on the verge of falling out of the community because of their economic distress. The community's responsibility to its diminished members is to "make them strong," restoring them to participation in community. The purpose of this empowerment is "that they may live *beside you* in the land." In Ps. 107:36 the hungry who receive God's steadfast love are able to "establish a town to live in." Once more they can be active, participating members of a community. The concern is for the person in community and what it takes to maintain the individual in that relationship.

Recognizing community participation as the key criterion has important consequences for understanding justice. Participation in community has multiple dimensions. Its spheres include physical life itself, political protection and decision making, social interchange and standing, economic production, education, culture, and religion. Community

---

13. Cf. Psalms 107; 113:7-9.
14. Cf. Jer. 23:5f.; 33:15f.

membership means the ability to share fully within one's capacity and potential in each essential aspect of community.

Justice provides the basic conditions for participation in community. These conditions provide the content of what is due in justice. They are the *deserts* of justice (to apply the category of what is deserved to a lack or deficiency rather than only as a corollary of some favorable attribute).

The conditions provided by justice are only a beginning. The receiving individuals have responsibility according to their ability to transform the conditions into the reality of the good life. For example, justice provides the conditions of religion through the freedom of religion, but it cannot produce genuine faith itself. There is a huge gap beyond justice in this case.

The concern for individuals as creatures of moral and spiritual worth before God is that they be active agents of their own well-being.[15] Anything less diminishes community membership. Justice provides the conditions to sustain that agency. When justice produces dependence (in contrast to mutuality), it has not been successful in completing its task. Its deliverance is incomplete. This is why the provision of land was so crucial in Israel's social economy. Land was a condition of agency that distribution of food itself could not provide. Land furnished membership in the economic community, while food ensured access only to the physical aspect of community life (itself a task of justice, however, when lacking).

From a deeper theological perspective, the basic claims of justice on members of the Hebrew community are to be understood in the light of God's universal justice, of God as creator of all, and of the death of Christ for all. The claims are then affirmed as valid for all people as members of the total human community.[16] The less universal communities that directly affect our everyday lives remain, nevertheless, crucial as the context for rights. Rights are the privileges of membership in the communities to which we belong.[17] Human rights, based in the universal

15. David Hollenbach, "The Common Good Revisited," *Theological Studies* 50 (1989): 92.

16. Cf. David Hollenbach, "A Communitarian Reconstruction of Human Rights: Contributions from Catholic Tradition" (a paper presented to Boston Theological Ethicists' Colloquium, October 17, 1990), p. 12. This essay will be published in a forthcoming book edited by Hollenbach and R. Bruce Douglass.

17. Max L. Stackhouse, *Creeds, Society, and Human Rights: A Study in Three Cultures* (Grand Rapids: Eerdmans, 1984), pp. 5, 44, 104f.

community, are those that must always be respected by the concrete communities to which we belong.

Basic Equality

Since membership in community involves a shared participation in all of its essential spheres, justice provides an equality in the fundamental elements of human life. Because of our common creator, masters are to grant "justice and equality" *(to dikaion kai tēn isotēta)* to their slaves (Col. 4:1, my translation). Equality before God is reflected in the same social requirements being placed on all of God's creatures, despite hierarchical differences among them (also Eph. 6:9); yet such categories of social status of the surrounding world are themselves challenged in light of God's singular majesty (Matt. 23:9) and the new creation brought into being by Christ (Gal. 3:28).[18]

What we mean by equality as a special component of biblical justice refers specifically to basic needs. Basic equality does not mean a mathematical division of all property and power or a leveling of all social goods. Basic needs are limited and capable of being defined. They are not infinite, so that anything that is apt to be desired in society is subject to just distribution. The first priority of distributive justice is to meet the basic needs of every member of the community.

The definition of *basic* needs cannot be stated in formulas applicable specifically and concretely in every case and to all times and cultures. But that does not make this theory of justice suspect. It means rather than it has sufficient flexibility to deal with varied experiences of human life. The need for elders in the gate to interpret the immediate meaning of justice continues. Debates about what is essential to community are proper, and both theological and empirical data are capable of providing guidance. Some matters apply to any culture, such as a basic protein requirement or security from torture. Other matters are relative to the demands of a culture. Access to motorized transportation is not basic where the institutions of the community are all within walking distance. But it *is* a basic need when the society is organized with the assumption that people have cars. These are not mystical or relativistic concerns, but rather contextual applications of basic principles.

18. Also Gal. 6:15; Col. 3:9-11; Eph. 2:14-16.

To be "needy" in this definition is to be involuntarily lacking in these resources. To treat Paul's statement that "anyone unwilling to work should not eat" (2 Thess. 3:10) as a theme for justice is to take it out of its context. Paul is addressing neither justice nor welfare. His concern is for those who, because of fanatical excitement about the return of Christ, have given up their everyday responsibilities. Although the purpose of work is to provide for the needy (Eph. 4:28), Paul did not regard those who were "unwilling to work" as truly needy because from his viewpoint they had the resources to care for themselves if they wished. Those who can provide for their basic needs but choose not to are not needy.

The compassion of justice, however, will see the presence of other needs if people appear capable of self-support but in contradiction to the normal self-interest accept the marginal life of welfare. The Bible's assumption is that when a needy person is encountered in the community the lack is due to external causes. Other information may alter that assumption. In the wisdom literature, particularly in Proverbs, when laziness is discussed, poverty in that context is often indicated as the consequence. The Deuteronomic warnings about unfaithfulness to God are similar.

In the Middle Ages when the ecclesiastical courts administered the welfare system as part of government, the principle was that a person able to work and not doing so was not needy and should not be provided for. Unlike today, there was not massive unemployment and that task of discernment was more simple. If such persons were close to perishing from want, however, they were to be provided for indifferently. Then they were manifestly needy. The canonists held that when in doubt it was better to do too much than to do nothing at all.[19] In addition, the dependents of such persons were often involuntarily deprived and proper subjects of community responsibility.

The principle of justice itself does not prevent unequal accumulations after the basic needs of all have been met. The biblical understanding of human nature, however, raises alarm at the potential for evil in sharp differences in power among individuals and groups in the society.

In biblical justice special attention is given to the weak so that they can realize along with all other members the minimum requirements of participation in the community. The Bible treats this principle

19. Brian Tierney, *Medieval Poor Law: A Sketch of Canonical Theory and Its Application in England* (Berkeley: University of California, 1959), pp. 58f.

in several ways. The most interesting and significant is the distribution of the land. The land, the common heritage from Yahweh, on which "all Israel" lived, from the greatest to the smallest,[20] was distributed impartially through specific legal guidance to the process of distribution (Numbers 16, Joshua 17).

The Jubilee functioned to perpetuate the arrangement of assuring productive property for each of the most basic economic units (Lev. 25:28). The concern was for a basic equality in productive property, and it required partiality in that those who had lost their land for a variety of reasons received access to them, and those who had gained these lands by whatever means lost it. The concern was for specific end results: participation in the economy by all and economic independence. Ezekiel prophesied a future restoration of this distribution of the land. The principle of that division was "you shall divide it equally" (Ezek. 47:14). Zech. 3:10 and Mic. 4:4 look to the time when once again all will sit under their own vine and fig tree, this representing security and access to means of production.

Benefit Rights as Well as Freedom Rights

Justice understood as access to all spheres essential to community requires a standard of justice for essential goods that are not in endless supply. The civil aspects of community, such as due process and forms of political participation, can be distributed to all without taking from others. Economic matters usually require some form of redistribution to set things right. Substantive justice, which grants benefit rights, accordingly is controversial because of its partiality.

Deliverance of the oppressed from the power of the strong in biblical justice, however, means action by the community that can be detrimental to the interests of the strong (e.g., Isa. 11:4). It may require adjustments in the community that, as in the Jubilee, take back productive property that was legitimately acquired.

Achieving justice may also involve provision of material essentials of life, such as food and shelter: God is the one "who executes justice [mišpāṭ] for the orphan and the widow, and who loves the strangers,

20. Cf. Hans Walter Wolff, *Anthropology of the Old Testament* (Philadelphia: Fortress, 1974), p. 187.

providing them food and clothing" (Deut. 10:18), "who executes justice for the oppressed; who gives food to the hungry" (Ps. 146:7; cf. 111:3-5; Job 8:6). "Food and clothing" is a Hebraism for what is indispensable.[21]

Job 24 describes the benefits that are taken away through injustice. Injustice starts with assault on the land, the basis of economic power (v. 2). It moves then to secondary means of production, the ass and the ox (v. 3). As a result the victims are characterized by powerlessness and indignity: The oppressors "thrust the poor off the road; the poor of the earth all hide themselves" (v. 4). The poor are separated from the bonds of community, wandering "like wild asses in the desert" (v. 5). They are dependent on others (v. 6). They are denied basic needs of food (vv. 6, 10), drink (v. 11), clothing, and shelter (vv. 7, 10). This loss of benefits is understood as injustice in other sections of Job as well.[22]

The connection of biblical justice to such material essentials of life in community stands in opposition to the conception of a purely negative function of government, in which government bears no responsibility for benefit rights. In such a view justice only prevents intrusions on the rights of others. It prevents, but does not provide. The rights that are protected are those of property, person, and equal access to the procedures of the community.

Negative Rights

The negative rights protected in that view are indeed crucial to justice. A person who is denied these protections is cut off from the political and civil community and is not only open to abuse, but is diminished in his or her ability to affect the life of the community. Remedial or criminal justice is critical to protect the individual or group from intrusions on their well-being. One example among many of retributive justice is the use of *mišpāṭ* for the judicial decision on one involved in involuntary taking of human life in Num. 35:12. The use of *mišpāṭ* in retributive justice is common. Procedural concerns are represented in concerns about just *(ṣedeq)* weights

---

21. C. Spicq, *Les Épîtres Pastorales* (Paris: Gabalda, 1969[4]), p. 190 (on 1 Tim. 6:8).

22. Cf. Job 22, where injustice includes the sins of omission of withholding drink from the weary and bread from the hungry (vv. 7, 23; cf. 31:17), as well as the exploitive use of economic power (v. 6a). In 31:19 the omission is failure to provide clothing.

and measures (Lev. 19:35f.), an emphasis in the prophetic and wisdom literature (e.g., Amos 8:5; Prov. 11:1). Due process is to be followed in judgment; there should be no bribes and neither the poor nor the rich are to be favored beyond their due claims (Deut. 16:19; Lev. 19:15).

The biblical conception of justice is foundational for such freedom rights, although our full understanding of them developed historically after the biblical period. They became more fully recognized as the experience of oppression was reflected on in the perspective of biblical insights into human depravity and human worth.

Positive Rights

But biblical justice also includes positive rights, which are the responsibility of the community. Rather than the neutral and only punitive image of the ruler, the true ruler is pictured as one who strengthens the weak, heals the sick, binds up the crippled, brings back the stray, and seeks the lost (Ezek. 34:4, 16, 23). Such an ideal ruler would take responsibility for the needs of the people as a shepherd. In Isa. 32:1-8, the promised just (v. 1) and wise king is contrasted to the fool who leaves the hungry unsatisfied (v. 6).

The justice required of the monarch and other rulers in the Bible cannot be distinguished in its quality and direction from the justice required of others. The concerns of government and law include a substantive, material, and benefit-oriented justice.

Because of its economic and social focus, rather than being merely civil, biblical justice has the continual association with groups such as widows, orphans, resident aliens, wage-earners, the poor, and slaves that we have noted. Justice responds to economic need.

Violations of civil and property rights are also frequently addressed. Economic deprivation often leads to vulnerability so that formal equality is perverted by substantive inequality. The situation, however, is not simply that members of these groups are denied equal civil process. If the concern were strictly a matter of violations of process and property, other groups also would be closely associated with justice. The most economically needy are not the only common victims of crime. Indeed, in such a situation of severe economic struggle the advantaged will be subject to crimes from the disadvantaged. "Give me neither poverty nor riches. . . . or I shall be poor, and steal" (Prov.

30:8f.). There is, however, no corresponding association of justice with wealthy groups or with other groups victimized only by crime (though biblical justice responds to these needs too).

The widow, orphan, and stranger stand out in the depth of their basic needs. Justice is closely connected to them because its theme is to meet basic needs so that all can be included in community. The needs to which it responds are civil and political, but also social and economic.

The Mosaic Law contains many benefit rights. The theory of justice of a culture cannot be interpreted apart from its legal system. Justice as an enforcement of this Law provided benefit rights. One of the distinctive characteristics of the Hebrew legal codes in the ancient Near East is their definite laws for relief of the poor.[23] The Law granted land to each extended family (Leviticus 25).[24] Food was a subject of several of its stipulations. The poor received food in the sabbatical year (Exod. 23:10f.) and in what was passed over in the first harvest (Deut. 24:19-22; Lev. 19:9f.). The hungry were to be allowed immediate consumption of food in the grainfields (Deut. 23:24f.). By a transfer payment, in every third year 10 percent of the harvest was put in storehouses in the towns for the poor (Deut. 14:28), a civil and public arrangement. It should be noted that there is no qualification in any of these texts stating that the poor people thus provided for are victims of criminal acts or illegal procedures. They merely are needy. One part of society is aided at a cost to other parts of society. Similarly, holding as security for a loan anything essential for life was proscribed as a matter of justice (ṣedaqâ, Deut. 24:13). The concern is not merely a process but concrete results. Benefits are given to the needy "so that they shall be satisfied" (Deut. 14:29; 23:24; 26:12).

Interest on consumptive loans was also prohibited as a harmful economic activity which threatened a person's community status (Lev. 25:35-37). A millstone was not to be used as security on a loan because as a person's productive property, it was that person's "life" (Deut. 24:6). In such cases, for the sake of consequences in basic needs, distributive justice interferes with what would otherwise be contracts "freely" entered into by both parties.

23. Norman W. Porteous, "The Care of the Poor in the Old Testament," in *Living the Mystery* (Oxford: Blackwell, 1967), p. 153.

24. Land is the provision of justice in Num. 27:5f. Moses brought before the Lord an appeal for justice (mišpāṭ, NRSV "case," v. 5) in land inheritance.

An Economic and a Legal Focus

The goal in restoration by justice is not to recover the integrity of the legal system as such. What is reestablished is the community as a place where the basic needs of all are met. The wrong to which justice responds is not merely an illegitimate process (like stealing). What is wrong is also an end result in which people are deprived of basic needs. "You shall not oppress (*'āšaq*) your neighbor or rob him" (Lev. 19:13).[25]

Certain forms of human relations are unjust in themselves even without consideration of the effects that they have on the lives of others. Stealing, cheating, and lying are immediately wrong and rightly restricted as much as possible by the law. Justice, however, also looks at situations in which people are deprived of what they need even if these intrinsically wrong actions are not present. Excessive power may take on the appearance of injustice only when it is perceived as having effects of depriving others of their rights.

Biblical oppression cannot be limited to the use of intrinsically wrong means to deprive others. Oppression occurs in any situation where unequal power leads to the denial of the basic needs of others, even if such results are not intentional or the means are not intrinsically evil. The process, such as foreclosing on lands put up as down payments on loans, may have been through valid and open contracts. The end result is condemned just as heavily and thus entitles government interference (Isa. 5:8; Neh. 5:1-7). Eryl Davies argues that Isaiah does not condemn as illegal the acquisition of the land denounced in Isa. 5:8-10. Through foreclosures of mortgages or through debt bondage, the property could be taken within the law.[26] Isaiah nevertheless condemns the rulers for not defending the weak. He appeals to social justice above the law, to which the law must respond. These prophetic themes serve as a warning against divorcing hunger from oppressive structures.

Justice concentrates on fulfilling basic unmet needs. Justice as

25. The following injunction in the second part of the verse against the practice of withholding the wages of a hired laborer until the next day illustrates the use of power to the disadvantage of one of the weakest groups in the community. The next verse goes on to deal with abuse of the blind.

26. Eryl W. Davies, *Prophecy and Ethics: Isaiah and the Ethical Traditions of Israel* (Sheffield: JSOT, 1981), pp. 69, 116.

deliverance also resists human forces that cause that deprivation. It responds not only to the oppressive use of excessive power,[27] but also to perversions or violations of the legal processes for similar ends. For the Bible injustice arises from the combination of power and greed.[28]

The ability of the poor to hold their own can be destroyed without the law being broken. In some situations of oppression there are great inequities in power and resources, and the poor have little control over their lives. They have little choice but to enter into debts, which are foreclosed without mercy. Buyers controlled by their competitors refuse to purchase a person's crops. A small farmer is outbid by the larger harvest offered to the buyer by his or her competitor. The owner of a small but profitable company is driven from business as his or her best workers leave for a larger company that offers them higher wages. That company may be less efficient but has broader resources to manipulate. Land reforms are thwarted when land is divided among relatives and lackeys who are only nominal owners so that the landholding oligarchy is able to maintain its dominant position.

The Bible gives attention to the content of justice or injustice — whether actions give life or destroy, rather than first of all to the question of legality or illegality. Restoration is not primarily to a legal position but to community. Justice is not a measure of conformity to whatever the law or contract may be. The standard of restoration is concerned with whether any social activity — legal, economic, social — brings people into supportive community or drives them out. Law is an effective and genuine social instrument as it gives expression to such justice.

Continuity with Love

Some argue that there are no benefit rights in justice under the assumption that justice and benevolence (or love) are separate principles. Benefits belong to love, not to justice. To claim benefits as rights is, in this view, to confuse love and justice. In addition, granting benefit rights also requires partiality in justice. Such partiality, it is said, belongs not to justice but to love, which is voluntary and does not include the work of the state.[29]

---

27. E.g., Amos 2:6f. and Job 22:6a.
28. Mic. 2:1f.; Eccl. 4:1.
29. E.g., Henry, *Aspects of Christian Social Ethics,* pp. 146-71.

Biblical justice, however, is frequently found in close association with love. As an example, love and justice in Deut. 10:18 are interchangeable: It is "the Lord" "who executes justice *[mišpāt]* for the orphan and the widow, and who loves the strangers, providing them food and clothing" (cf. Isa. 30:19).[30]

Not all benevolence is justice; nevertheless, love that responds to basic unmet material needs legitimately calls forth justice. Such a loving, benevolent type of justice is not a confusion about biblical justice. It is the meaning of distributive justice in the Scriptures.

One can understand why Paul used language drawn from the sphere of distributive justice to describe God's salvation through Christ. This language was already associated with salvation. It spoke of actions of deliverance of those who had no other recourse and could not help themselves, actions of bringing people back into community. Paul uses the major Greek term for justice, *dikaiosynē*, which corresponded to ṣedaqâ, one of the two major Hebrew words for justice, to describe the creative power that brings God's gift of salvation and opens the way into the redeemed community that God is forming (e.g., Rom. 1:16f.). It is in contrast to God's retributive justice, in the form of *wrath* (v. 18), from which Christ provides deliverance. Paul refers to the *dikaiosynē* ("righteousness") of God particularly in Romans, where he defends God's actions in bringing the Gentiles into the household of God through faith in Christ.[31]

Paul's usage is metaphorical, as is all language referring to God. Therefore, not all aspects of justice can be pressed from the term *dikaiosynē*. (It is also invalid to attempt to read the entire meaning of atonement into this term.) The perspective in Paul's use of *dikaiosynē* is on God's grace and love in bringing those without claims to community into community. The grounds are arbitrarily established by God's completely unmerited favor. Only faith in Christ is the ground for this community. Only God's grace supplies the ability to respond in faith. Once God has established it, however, faith is a claim that God promises

30. On justice as a continuation of the meaning of love, see S. C. Mott, *Biblical Ethics and Social Change* (New York: Oxford University, 1982), pp. 61-64. For examples of the association of justice with love or grace beyond what is supplied there, see Pss. 36:5f.; 40:10; 89:14-17; 111:3f.; 112:4-6; 116:5-7; 119:149, 156; 143:11f.; 145:7-9, 17; Isa. 63.7f. LXX.

31. Cf. Marcus Barth, "Jews and Gentiles: The Social Character of Justification in Paul," *Journal of Ecumenical Studies* 5 (1968): 241-67.

to recognize. God brings into God's community all who have faith, no matter their wretchedness and previous lack of standing in the community. God's *dikaiosynē* cuts through the false and excluding status privileges of works and nationality (Rom. 3:21-31).

It is not valid to argue back from this usage of this term to establish the meaning of social justice. It is confirming, however, to see the continuity of meaning in the justice terms applied to the salvific work of Christ.

Distribution according to Needs in Community

The description of biblical justice must take into account all these factors: its focus on economic weakness, deliverance, and restoration, the social priority of basic needs and of participation in community, legal support of benefit rights as well as rights of protection and procedure, and the continuity of justice with love.

Among the traditional formulas of distributive justice the one most appropriate in describing biblical justice is distribution according to needs. These needs include both benefits and procedures and are oriented to life in community. Some of the other criteria of distributive justice are at least assumed. Within these confines, there is a place for achievement (or ability) and contract.

When the biblical writers are intentional about justice, however, and are using justice terminology, it is distribution according to needs that prevails. This is the central direction for the conduct of the distributive systems. This intentionality about justice is not present in the narratives of great wealth for some individuals nor in legal provisions that assume the existence of slavery. When justice is set forth, it is the basic needs for inclusion in community that are set forth; and these concerns give direction to the economic, social and legal ordering of the community.

Information, Values, and Government Action

Peter J. Hill

How useful is it for Christians who have fundamental disagreements over matters of economic policy to spend time discussing those disagreements with one another? Will such interaction exacerbate the differences and create bitterness, or will substantive healing occur and useful insights into areas of agreement be forthcoming? As those of us who participated in Oxford I and Oxford II look back at that process, it is now time to engage in serious reflection on what went on so that we might be good stewards as we contemplate future dialogue.

I must confess that I entered the entire Oxford process somewhat skeptically. I longed for contact with my brothers and sisters in Christ and for fruitful dialogue with those with whom I had disagreements. However, I was not sure that trying to reach agreement on a general statement would be that useful, and I also feared that our differences might be so great that we would not truly listen to one another. But the process certainly revealed that I was in error. Useful dialogue did occur, people did listen seriously to one another, learning from each other, and modification of positions did result; the final Oxford Declaration served a useful purpose in forcing us to articulate our positions and look for areas of commonality.

The final document did not represent just empty rhetoric, an attempt to mask differences with ambiguous wording. The process indicated important areas of agreement and also was very useful to participants who found that listening to others revealed their own blind spots or areas of insensitivity that had been overlooked. It was interesting to see some members from the left agree that inflation and protectionism were truly significant problems with negative impacts on the poor. On the other side, participants who were more sympathetic to markets agreed that the culture of capitalism can be decidedly non-Christian and that there can be undue concentrations of wealth and power under markets. Thus the dialogue was extremely helpful in expanding the vision of the participants and pointing out areas of commonality of concern that most of them shared.

Given that the dialogue was in its first stages, the degree of agreement was encouraging. It was very useful to find unifying goals that need to be striven for through economic policy and to identify areas of concern as one uses either market mechanisms or government to achieve these goals. It is now probably time to move beyond these unifying perspectives and to talk more specifically about particular policies and reforms.

Although I found the past process to be an exhilarating experience in discovering areas of agreement and in learning from other Christians, I am not so optimistic that future dialogue will be as productive in producing agreement. As we move into the realm of specific policies, I expect that we will discover that we have substantial differences about "how the world works." Another way of expressing that is to say that we might have vastly different estimates of the costs and consequences of trying to achieve certain of the goals that we have outlined. In the rest of this chapter, I will detail where I think the future debate should go and where we will find substantial differences of opinion. This is done not to sabotage any future efforts of dialogue but rather, in the spirit of Oxford I and Oxford II, with the hope of enhancing serious reflection and discussion on the issues.

Although any attempt to classify Christians concerned about economic policy is fraught with problems, I will place people in two camps, those who might be called pro-market and those who are much more distrustful of market processes. For ease of explication, I will label the two competing groups as noninterventionists and interventionists, though I recognize that such terminology does not always accurately describe a person's position on a particular issue. Of course it is only fair to be frank and acknowledge that I belong in the first category.

Noninterventionists would be much more inclined to favor the use of prices and property rights as the major coordinating devices for society, while interventionists would be more suspicious of markets and would argue that government needs to be a very active agent in inter-

101

vening to ameliorate many of the consequences of market forces. Of course, people are located along a continuum with regard to these positions and it is easy to caricature the extremes on both ends. Very few of the pro-market advocates are calling for removal of all government; by the same token, few of the pro-government group believe that central control and planning should replace the market on all margins. Nevertheless, there are serious differences between the two basic camps and it is worth examining these disagreements. My thesis is that those differences are more at the level of perceptions of how different policies play out rather than in substantial disagreements over fundamental values.[1] I believe that there are very different views of how easy it is to achieve certain policy goals and the degree to which we face constraints and trade-offs in implementing those goals. I now turn to several questions that I think illustrate substantial differences in views about the reality of the world we operate in and that would have been more evident had we moved beyond the somewhat general statements of Oxford II.

Are Good Intentions Enough?

Fundamental to many of the statements in the Oxford Declaration is the view that the major reason for social evils is the lack of good intentions on the part of members of society. Thus numerous statements call for a greater sense of obligation to high ideals and a deeper moral commitment to certain principles of justice. If people's level of moral awareness can be raised, social problems can be solved.

Surely intentions are important for Christians as they debate matters of public policy. However, there is an issue of causality hidden in some of these statements. The noninterventionists believe that unintended consequences play a major role in government actions, while the interventionists believe such consequences play a minor role. Therefore, for the noninterventionists, resolving the matter of intentions will not necessarily solve all of our problems. For instance, why are many economists critical of minimum wage legislation? Because elementary

---

1. An exception to this statement is in the area of defining biblical justice. It became clear at Oxford II that there were fundamental differences among the participants as to what justice is, and these differences were left largely unresolved.

102

economic analysis tells us that increases in the minimum wage will probably increase the unemployment rate of the unskilled, a consequence certainly unintended by many who advocate such legislation.

If many of the social problems we observe are not intentional results of human action, then solving those problems involves more than simply raising the level of moral commitment. To build a social policy exclusively around the hope of changed hearts is fraught with danger. Focusing primarily on the level of moral and spiritual commitment in a society may cause us to ignore other important constraints on human behavior.

Some of the discussions of poverty in the Oxford II statement imply that such poverty is the most unnatural of conditions and results largely from the bad intentions of individuals. It is true that in the garden of Eden poverty was not present. However, in our present fallen world it is not clear that we can resolve poverty problems by simply making people better intended. If the people of Bangladesh became less greedy would the country become wealthy? Probably not. Neither would a sharp reduction in materialism by Americans necessarily result in prosperity for the peasants of Bangladesh. Capital accumulation and wealth generation are necessary to overcome poverty. Economic growth requires an appropriate institutional setting and a specific set of cultural attitudes toward work, risk, savings, and personal responsibility. We should not assume that the reduction of selfish behavior automatically creates the appropriate conditions for the creation of wealth.

How Available Is Information?

Many of the interventionists appear confident that the requisite information is at hand to make better decisions — if only people wanted to make better decisions. They also tend to believe that the information generated by private property rights and markets is fundamentally flawed. The fact that sin mars our choices is seen as ample reason for distrusting individual evaluations as expressed in relative prices for consumer goods and for life and health. Instead, information should come from alternative sources. These sources are usually not specified since it is assumed that we are dealing with knowledge that is easily available to all concerned.

In the view of these Christians, since sin mars individual choices there needs to be a social mechanism for assessing high-priority and low-priority needs and then building social policy around the high priority needs. The process for determining the most important needs is not clearly specified, but the general assumption seems to be that the process itself is not important since it is so clearly obvious which needs fall into which category. It is also assumed that society can reach general agreement quite easily on the relevant classifications so that little conflict would be generated in reaching appropriate conclusions.

The degree to which each set of needs is to be met is also not specified. But any effort actually to identify and fulfill high-priority needs would immediately run into trouble. Should all high-priority needs be met before any low-priority needs are allowed to be satisfied? Can people attend amusement parks in a society where there is a shortage of kidney dialysis machines? Does strawberry cheesecake satisfy a high- or a low-priority need? These questions are not raised to trivialize the argument about needs, but rather because judgments about those issues will be required if collective decisions are used to allocate goods on the basis of a ranking of needs.

Markets are important information-generating networks. They provide a feedback mechanism for participants and an authentication process to determine the validity of knowledge. They do not process information perfectly, nor should Christians automatically accept all market signals as valid for individual choices. However, it is difficult to conceive of a just economic policy that replaces the information generated by markets with a social consensus on high- and low-priority needs. If we replace markets with any alternative social coordination mechanism, it will probably be somewhat impersonal and will also probably not provide adequate information for all decisions. Therefore we ought to be careful about formulating policy on the assumption that the information necessary for effective policy implementation is readily available.

Does Injustice Always Require Collective Action?

Justice is an important concept for both the interventionists and the noninterventionists. However, the noninterventionists see complete justice as very difficult to attain and therefore are more willing to trade some justice for other social goals. Under their view of the world, justice may be best achieved by general rules, recognizing that such rules in some particular applications will lead to injustice. The interventionists have much more faith in instituting particularized justice and believe that evidence of cases of injustice provide ample reason for social reform. However, even if there is agreement that certain situations do represent injustice, it does not follow that collective action should be taken to remedy that injustice. To render such judgments successfully requires a large amount of information, information that may not be readily available. Likewise, one must always ask, can such an exacting standard be applied without causing other injustices of even greater magnitude?

From the perspective of the noninterventionists, it is important to recognize that God's standard of perfect justice does exist, but also that the omniscient God is in a much better position to implement divine judgments than we are. That does not mean that we should not seek to understand God's standards and apply them when possible. But it does mean that we must understand the limits that our own fallibility places on us in implementing those standards.

One area where this fallibility is particularly significant is in constructing policy to achieve a just income distribution. The calls to justice in the Oxford Declaration could be interpreted as assuming that it is not difficult to determine quite precisely who deserves what and that it is also fairly easy to construct policy to see that everyone gets their just deserts. However, in reality it is very difficult to sort out the reasons for income differences. Some result from voluntary choices with regard to education, family size, preferences for leisure and certain types of labor, and attitudes toward risk, while others are not the direct result of the choices of the individuals involved. Surely such information is important in implementing a just income redistribution policy, and any attempt to alter incomes to achieve a more just distribution through large-scale government action must face the fact that such efforts can result in grave injustices.

Part of the confusion over the application of standards of justice stems from a failure to recognize differences in costs of information at different levels of action. A family may be able to apply a very individualized standard of justice because family members can obtain reasonably good information about the abilities and intentions of each other. Likewise, the local community of believers may also use personalized criteria for judging situations that make allowances for particular circumstances and events in each person's life. However, as the group under consideration becomes larger and there is less of a shared purpose among its members, such particularized justice becomes more difficult to institute. Thus as one attempts to remedy injustice at higher levels of government, adequate information may not be available to formulate policies that promote justice.

Another danger with use of large-scale government intervention to achieve particularized justice is that the coercive power necessary to achieve such goals can be badly used and can violate other justice concerns. For example, it is true that people are unjustly fired from jobs. However, a government policy that requires review of all hiring and firing decisions and provides easy access to legal remedies for "unjust" firings represents a substantial diminution of the sphere of freedom for individuals and groups in ordering their own lives. Under such a program can Christian schools fire homosexual teachers? Can Christian employers favor people who share their faith? Probably not. The world may be more just if government simply enforces employment contracts and prevents misrepresentation and fraud.

How Effective Is Government?

The participants in Oxford II found government to be both a potential source of oppression and a way of relieving oppression. It is difficult to determine from the Oxford Declaration whether one should be wary of government or should see it as a useful mechanism for alleviating social ills. However, as specific policy proposals are debated it is easy to predict that there will be fundamental differences in views about the efficacy of government. Interventionists are much more likely to trust government to solve problems and to institute justice.

On the other hand, noninterventionists tend to be suspicious of government because of their fear that its power will be inappropriately used and that special-interest groups will be able to bend government to serve their own ends.

These fundamental differences are illustrated by differing perspectives on the usefulness of government in combating the problem of concentrations of economic power in market societies. Interventionists believe that a more active government policy can be helpful in reducing concentrations of power. On the other hand, noninterventionists are much more likely to find government itself the source of the concentration of power through licensing, protective tariffs, and other regulations. Thus their solution is to reduce the sphere of government in order to make society more open. In contrast, interventionists would expand the sphere of government to offset private concentrations of economic power.

In conclusion, as the debate among Christians continues about appropriate economic policies, it may be more difficult to secure agreement as we move to the more specific level of policy proposals. I have suggested that there is general agreement on certain goals that a just society should be striving to achieve, but also that there are very different perspectives about the likelihood of achieving those goals. This is not to argue that further dialogue will be useless, but rather that we ought to be realistic as we enter into future discussions. There are some very substantial differences in conceptions of "how the world works," over what trade-offs there are between certain goals, and over the costliness of achieving particular ends. Fortunately, many of these issues can be at least partially resolved by serious discussion and by examination of evidence from around the world. We as Christians must continue to seek common ground, but we must not gloss over our differences regarding the likelihood of success of certain policies and the effects of particular reforms.

Destroying Poverty without Destroying Poor People

Herbert Schlossberg

What the Oxford Declaration Missed

It is astonishing that the Oxford Declaration on Christian Faith and Economics, the consensus document from Oxford II, says virtually nothing about capital formation. This in spite of a good statement on the creation and stewardship, which is the foundation of all capital and its proper use. And also in spite of the presence of a number of people, including myself, whose orientation could have been expected to flag such an absence. It seems to be one of those cases in which the trees are so interesting that the absence of an important portion of the forest goes unnoticed. This omission becomes more understandable when we contemplate Oxford I. Although billed as an economic conference, its real subject was poverty. Most of the participants assumed that a discussion of economics is really a discussion of poverty; that may be why Oxford I accomplished so little.

That kind of mind-set became so ingrained that the customary attacks on capitalism — and the more common delegitimation of it by eliciting fear for its "victims" — at Oxford I did not speculate on the source of the replacement capital should that dreaded institution be swept away. This question is of central importance because without capital there can be no economic life, whether under capitalism, socialism, some hybrid between the two, or whatever alternative might be conjured up by the imagination. If we regard capital in its most basic sense as anything that produces a continuing stream of benefits, then it becomes clear that personal and physical assets will always be essential to economic life. And something is going to be used to allocate those assets to one use or the other. If it is not done by free people using markets, then it will be done by politicians and bureaucrats using compulsion. The only alternative to the allegedly terrible Invisible Hand is the much more terrible Iron Fist.

Thus in the Declaration of Oxford II we have a significant oversight. But that dark cloud has an exceedingly important silver lining in that the Declaration also formally endorsed the income generating study presented at the conference by its author, Professor Joe Remenyi, an economist at Deakin University in Australia. Moreover, the conference endorsed the publication of the study in book form, a project that was successfully completed.[1] Therefore we can legitimately consider the Remenyi study's position on capital as part of the Oxford Declaration. Unfortunately, this study deals only with a very small part of both the issue and the Oxford mandate, dealing as it does only with capital formation among very poor people. Still, that is valuable in its own right and worthy of study and reflection.

And it comes just in time. I would guess that the general befuddlement on this subject is as great as we will find on any important issue. And evangelicals have contributed as much as any group to the self-defeating ignorance, so blatant that it appears almost willful. One scholar, in a book published by a press of the student evangelical movement in the United States, writes that the idea that wealth can be created is a "deceptive myth." Wealth cannot be created, he says. "It can only be accumulated or redistributed."[2] The reader can judge this astonishing statement in the light of the findings of the Remenyi study. Let it suffice for the moment to say that this is an unconscious call for class warfare, based on an envy-driven demand for the property of others, since nothing we want and believe we should have can be obtained by any means except to take it from someone else. Evidently the writer believes that the amount of capital now present in, say, Massachusetts is about the same as it was when English feet first stepped on Plymouth Rock.

The reason some people can find such nonsense plausible is that they do not know why they are not poor. They know the bromides: "Work hard, save your money, and you'll get ahead." Like most bodies

---

1. Joe Remenyi, *Where Credit Is Due* (London: Intermediate Technology, 1990).
2. Howard A. Snyder, *A Kingdom Manifesto: Calling the Church to Live Under God's Reign* (Downers Grove: InterVarsity, 1985), p. 103.

of conventional wisdom such maxims are more or less correct. But they do not go far enough. They do not account for the cultural and institutional factors that have made western prosperity possible. In literature like the Remenyi report we are able to see how even poor people can create capital and attain economic vitality.

Remenyi's Study

The "income generation" with which the Remenyi study deals is the activity of nongovernmental organizations (NGOs) in lending small amounts of money to poor people who invest it in productive economic enterprises. These small businesses typically are tiny fabricating or food processing operations or retail outlets. Many of them are conducted in the rude shelters that house the loan recipients. With the borrowed money the entrepreneurs usually buy stock for resale or for processing into finished goods. The loans are typically very small, often less than $100. NGOs set up repayment schedules that are appropriate to the scale of the project and the capabilities of the borrower. Often these schedules require payments to be made on a daily basis.

Studies have shown varying but good to spectacular results among many of these organizations. In Bangladesh the modal rate of return of two-thirds of the organizations studied was 50 percent per year. Another study of eighteen NGOs in Bangladesh showed annual rates of return between 50 percent and 250 percent. In India the average increase in income from 631 small loans was 60 percent. World Vision India had an average increase in income from 150 small loans of more than 160 percent per year. In the Philippines, the average increase in income was 41 percent from loans averaging $94 in size. Again in the Philippines the average increase in income among 7,089 borrowers was 33 percent, with an average loan amount of $112. In Java, Indonesia, savings by group members doubled within a year. In Peru the average increase in income from 6,200 loans was 29 percent per year; in Costa Rica, the average increase in income from 450 small loans was more than 100 percent per year and there was one new job created for every $1000 loaned. These figures are extraordinarily high because the community of poverty suffers so much from underinvestment. As this is mitigated we can expect the growth in income figures to move down and become much closer to what we expect from commercial banking activities.

The term Remenyi uses for the enterprises to which the NGOs loan their funds is *Credit-Based Income Generating Projects* (CB-IGPs). He found three broad types in operation, with various permutations of each. The first he calls the personal integrity model. This is a minimalist operation of pure credit; one type lends money to individuals, another to an umbrella group that does a lot of the administrative work — for example, an association of automobile recyclers in Indonesia. A second type is the savings-linked credit group. This model mobilizes savings by poor people as an important component of its program, and lends the money to members of the group as working capital. Sometimes the individual is part of a solidarity group which imposes social discipline and makes default of the loan more unlikely. There is also the welfare-oriented credit model. This also has minimalist techniques but is more oriented toward community transformation, often with a paid "change agent" to make things happen. Community development is the main goal, with the provision of credit subordinate. This includes "empowerment" and consciousness-raising, and some varieties of it treat poor people as needing the services of others on a continuing basis. Organizations based on this model have a moral hazard built into them, with many opportunities for kickbacks, thievery, and excessive transaction costs.

The benefits of these loans are greater than the obvious one that poor people have their incomes raised. Since the entrepreneurs' customers are to a large extent their neighbors, poor communities have better access to goods and services; and to the extent that competition is increased prices will be lowered. Many income generating projects have made multiple loans to the same borrowers as their businesses grow and take on employees. Thus professional development of both the entrepreneurs and the people they hire takes place. This increases the social capital of the poor community. On a level that is harder to demonstrate, the visible increase in vitality and social health shows people that their own efforts can avail in difficult circumstances, thus making the siren call of envy and resentment that come from ever-present demagogues easier to resist.

Those intangibles are too readily spurned in a world that is almost unconsciously materialistic, and it is one of the strengths of the Remenyi study that he recognizes them. He is very hard on the "top-down" programs that have a much higher failure rate than the ones that deliberately rely on community participation. This is an especially im-

111

portant factor when the loan size is small because the transaction cost of each loan can be such a high proportion of the loan value. A $100 loan simply could not be made if the processing expense were anything like that of a lending institution in the formal sector. The solution is for the community of the borrower to pick up the transaction costs that otherwise would fall on the lender. In fact Remenyi believes that one way of judging whether a process is top-down (bad) or bottom-up (good) is whether the transaction costs are internalized by the lending agency or picked up by the community. When I visited an NGO in the Philippines that was part of Remenyi's study I saw a small grocery store in a poor neighborhood — itself a multiple loan recipient — acting as a collection agency for the NGO, serving the small entrepreneurs of the area. As people came in with their daily loan payments, the transactions would be entered into the books, and the NGO then had only to deal with the one store; thus the transaction costs were lowered dramatically, making the program much more viable. All this is in addition to the greater efficiencies of the market-driven economies of the small businesses, inherently far more able to pick up economic signals from the economy than would a central bureaucracy. And there is a further payoff in the increase of a sense of dignity and worth that the entrepreneur has in not being expected meekly to follow orders from a loan officer or bureaucrat.

One fact that ought to be emphasized is that the process Remenyi describes is not charity, although almost all of the money expended is derived ultimately either from charitable giving, usually from Christian groups, or tax money funneled through the NGOs. Poor entrepreneurs are able to pay market rates of interest, and that is the normal policy of the NGOs. Interest and principal payments, of course, are recycled through the credit program for use in other projects. The problem with the formal credit system is not the interest rate but the unavailability of credit at any price. One reason that the rate of repayment of these loans is so high — often close to 100 percent — is that once the poor gain access to credit they will go to almost any length to keep it.

There is a great payoff in job creation. Economic activity in the informal economy is labor intensive, and therefore a small investment can pay big dividends in providing work opportunities. One survey among small artisans in Nairobi revealed that the average job required an investment of $15.37. Even in wealthy countries job creation is much more a function of small enterprises than of large ones. It has become a commonplace that the enormous job-generating accomplishment of the U.S. in the last twenty years — compared with a static job-creation scene in western Europe — is due to the small-business sector. New companies appear because of the effect of past savings. People invest their own money, or the savings of friends and relatives, and use spare space in basements, garages, and extra bedrooms — another form of savings. These savings are unavailable to comparable entrepreneurs in poor communities. So the CB-IGP serves to level the playing field between comparable people in different economic circumstances.

In general, the record of foreign aid establishments, both national and international, has been abysmal, partly because of the phenomenon that Remenyi explains in his top-down, bottom-up schema. I do not believe this will ever change, because the political process will always tend to favor those who have a *quid pro quo* to offer, which by definition does not include poor people. But there are exceptions. The International Fund for Agricultural Development is a small United Nations agency that makes small loans to groups of villagers. National governments are bypassed, which means that the opportunities for corruption and waste are greatly reduced. Recipients are people who would not be considered credit-worthy by banks, and there is no collateral required. Loans are made to small groups of people who know each other and who share liability, so there is group pressure to repay since no one wants to lose face. A bank in Bangladesh is trying the same thing, and has a repayment rate of 99 percent. One in Mali has a repayment rate of 100 percent. A group in Honduras has a repayment rate of 85 to 90 percent.[3] Similar attempts have been made in the United States,[4] but there the welfare mentality has so taken root, with both

3. *The Economist,* August 20, 1989, p. 70.
4. See, e.g., David Osborne, "A Poverty Program that Works," *The New Republic,* May 8, 1989, pp. 22-25. This program is the Shorebank Corporation in Chicago's South Shore neighborhood. It is subsidized by philanthropists but encompasses a change of culture. It is a business and will go under if it makes bad investments, so it chooses carefully the people it will back. They have to know what they are doing and have commitment. Its weakness is that while it pays for itself it is not profitable enough to get others to replicate its success. So its backers believe government investment is necessary, a mistake that will do the most to ensure its failure. The program began by financing the purchase of rundown housing to poor people who rehabilitated it with their labor, some learning Spanish in order to communicate with tenants. The program included training and business development efforts. In 1988, their best year, almost no real estate loans went bad and even commercial loans did well. The backers are trying the same thing in a depressed rural area in Arkansas.

recipients and politically powerful ideological forces and vested interests propping it up, that it is difficult to gain support for an alternative, no matter what improvement might be brought by it.

The Importance of Cultural Capital

Remenyi says that there is no formula or recipe that can yield success for CB-IGPs. Rather, what is needed are hard work, dedication, common sense, honesty, integrity, and the ability to learn from experience. Very true. These are all cultural traits, and Remenyi thus puts himself in the camp of those, such as the University of London development economist P. T. Bauer, who stress the importance of culture for economic performance.[5] But then Remenyi says: "Most of that wisdom is in the hands of the poor themselves. . . . The very first and most fundamental 'secret' is, therefore, not to spurn the poor, but to recognize in them an asset that is the foundation of sustainable success." To the extent that this counsel is not to patronize the people that one is supposed to be helping, it is certainly good advice. But there is no recognition in it that the lack of economic performance may be only partly an institutional problem and therefore cannot be addressed successfully by credit facilities alone. And even within the institutional realm it may never be possible to achieve much more than nibbling away at the margins without measures that lie far beyond the scope of NGOs and neighborhood entrepreneurial activities. The participants in Oxford II were intrigued by a report on the work of Hernando de Soto, who shows the shocking state in which the statist mentality of his native Peru has left the poor masses, who can do practically nothing legally, so slanted toward the pressures of the rich has the energy of the state been directed.[6]

5. See the various works of P. T. Bauer, especially *Dissent on Development: Studies and Debates in Development Economics* (London: Weidenfeld and Nicolson, 1971). Two other books by Bauer are also useful: *Reality and Rhetoric: Studies in the Economics of Development* (Cambridge: Harvard University, 1984) and *Equality: The Third World and Economic Delusion* (Cambridge: Harvard University, 1981). For a brief study of Bauer's work and significance see Herbert Schlossberg, "The Free Economy: P. T. Bauer's Empirical Analysis," in *Freedom, Justice, and Hope: Toward a Strategy for the Poor and the Oppressed,* ed. Marvin Olasky (Westchester: Crossway, 1988), pp. 85-98.

6. Hernando de Soto, *The Other Path: The Invisible Revolution in the Third World,* tr. June Abbott (New York: Harper and Row, 1989).

Government policies commonly take away the fruits of hard work and economic success by jailing, confiscations, taxation, and extortion. Such events take place in many of the countries that Remenyi visited. And it is often attitudes toward work, family, physical reality, and other values to which Remenyi calls attention that are lacking, thus preventing people from rising out of poverty. The lesson in this is that institutional and cultural factors are like the thumb working together with the fingers of more narrowly economic factors: There can be no closure unless the apposite digits are functioning normally and cooperatively.

The purpose of the CB-IGPs described in Remenyi's study is to alleviate poverty. If there are three legs to this particular stool — the provision of financial liquidity, a condition of minimal justice to allow people to prosper and to keep the fruit of their economic progress, and a reasonably healthy culture (that is, extramaterial factors) — then placing all the stress on only one of the three will not avail as much as it appears to avail in this study. We know from abundant experience — including material in the Remenyi study — that pouring money into a social situation can mean absolutely nothing in terms of economic health. If the culture cannot use the money productively or if the government destroys the infrastructure of justice, then the capital is soon gone, leaving the community in the same or worse state.

Remenyi touches on such issues, but he does not focus squarely on them. For example, he mentions a study of twenty-five very large World Bank projects that concluded that an important variable is the development of grassroots organizations to enable the beneficiaries to assume increasing responsibility for the projects that sustained them. But Remenyi's commentary on this study does not address the issue of the project being so conducted as to increase the capacity of the recipients to make increasingly better use of liquidity.

Economic analyses often regard cultural capital as fixed, with financial liquidity the only kind of capital needed by poor people. The assumption seems to be that moral and cultural capital either are irrelevant to the issue or else are a fixed quantity that one can safely ignore. To a suggestion that physical capital is a fixed quantity, the economist would protest that everything we know about economics debunks that notion. Assuming that cultural capital is so fixed will not do, especially in a consideration of economic matters by Christians.

This issue has been commonly mistaken by proponents of redistribution, but advocates of the free market also often underestimate the cultural determinants of economic prosperity. Michael Novak's review of Peter Berger's well-received book *The Capitalist Revolution: Fifty Propositions About Prosperity, Equality, and Liberty,* although very favorable, is critical of Berger's underestimation of culture, a fault Novak believes is typical of sociologists. Novak says we have to consider that there cannot be private property without respect for law, markets without respect for contracts, enterprise without confidence in creative practical intellect, or investments without willingness to defer reward.[7] *Respect, law, confidence, intellect,* and *willingness to defer* are all cultural terms denoting qualities that cannot be imparted by the mere provision of credit.

This kind of analysis is almost entirely absent not only from the Remenyi study but also from the Oxford Declaration. That is true in spite of the paper that I read on this issue at Oxford II.[8] But the participants in the conference apparently were not convinced that nonmaterial determinants of economic life are important. I do not believe there were more than a handful of Marxists present at the conference, if that, and yet the Marxist dogma that economics is based wholly on material factors held sway as far as the Declaration is concerned. The Declaration specifically stated that the Bible was the basis for the conference's understanding of economic life, but in this area at least that intention was not matched by the performance. If it had been, some attention would have been given to the promises and curses of Deuteronomy 28, to cite only one passage among multitudes:

> If you will only obey the Lord your God. . . . Blessed shall be . . . the fruit of your ground, and the fruit of your livestock, both the increase of your cattle and the issue of your flock. . . . But if you will not obey the Lord your God. . . . Cursed shall be . . . the fruit of your ground, the increase of your cattle and the issue of your flock (vv. 1, 4, 15, 18).

That Remenyi does not make much of cultural issues in describing the activities of CB-IGPs should not be taken to mean such issues are not important in the projects he studied. He reports that many of the

---

7. *The American Spectator,* August 1986, pp. 41-44.
8. Entitled "The Cultural Roots of Economic Development."

recipients are approved on the basis of the recommendations of pastors, but he does not say much more about this. What criteria do the pastors use in deciding whether or not to recommend approval? What are the effects of this selection process on the makeup of the corps of recipients? Is it reasonable to suppose that applicants who are habitually lazy, dishonest, improvident, antisocial, blasphemous, unfaithful, ignorant, or drunk will routinely slip through the screening process and be awarded loans? And if the process, although informal and cheap to administer, as Remenyi notes, nevertheless is effective at skewing the loans toward those best able to use them successfully, then there is a rather fine net that is scooping out of the entrepreneurial waters the mass of those who do not possess the qualities necessary to succeed there.

When I visited one of the NGOs that Remenyi studied, the manager opened a door and showed me a dozen or so potential entrepreneurs in a seminar designed to imbue them with just those qualities, including the biblical virtues, they needed to succeed. Evidently K. W. Taylor, chairman of the Oxford Conference committee that directed the study, felt the need for more consideration of such matters. In his separate paper on the role of evangelism and the impartation of Christian values, he shows the relationship of both to economic life. For example, he quotes from a statement of one of the NGOs, the Bridge Foundation in Pakistan:

> In our training seminars as well as personal consultancy to the clients, we emphasize the value of doing the right thing in all areas of the business: to offer the best services to the customer, to deal with competition healthily and to pay taxes whenever due. In short, we promote the practices of the right business ethics in a climate where dishonesty, corruption and expediency are the rule. Our screening and evaluation procedures are geared to identifying clients who subscribe to as many of these values as possible.[9]

Taylor says that even though it is absent in the official reports, Christian witness is having an important effect. He cites anecdotal evidence to show the effects of evangelism and of instruction in "stewardship of

9. K. W. Taylor, "The Role of Evangelism, Christian Values, and Christian Community," p. 8.

the Lord's resources, seeking God first in all we do before anything else, and so on."[10]

To say that most people in poor countries do not possess whatever it takes for an entrepreneur to succeed is not to disparage them. Few people *any* place have the requisite skills and qualities. As a failed entrepreneur, I speak from some experience. Surely the biblical doctrines of gifts and callings should lead us to suspect that not many are likely to succeed in *any* one given occupation, including entrepreneurship, but only those whose gifts prepare them for that occupation. Nonetheless, as Remenyi rightly emphasizes, there is a ripple effect of the small corps of entrepreneurs in a poor community. They provide goods and services that either would not exist without them or at prices that would be higher, they employ people who would not otherwise be employed, they keep money within the community that otherwise would be siphoned out, they energize community life in ways that only commercial activity can do, and they provide hope among their peers, examples of success for others to emulate.

Treating Poor People with Dignity

One of the most galling attributes of many who appear to bask in the glow of their own compassion is their damnable patronizing of poor people. And one of the refreshing aspects of Remenyi's paper is that he does not indulge himself in this vice. Poor people do not need subsidies, he says, and he argues for the advantages of not giving any.

> The poor live in the school of hard knocks and value nothing more than being treated with dignity and justice. . . . It is a pleasure to them when they receive value for money and are not denied access. . . . They will willingly pay for services and technical assistance that [are] perceived as relevant and fairly priced, and are more than happy to pay interest rates that are at market levels.

In other words poor people are neither children nor congenital idiots, and in place of the ersatz compassion that often not only dehumanizes them but uses them to advance extraneous and usually damaging ideo-

10. *Ibid.,* p. 5.

118

logical purposes, we should show them the real article. Poor people, like the rest of us, have strengths and weaknesses, have among their number saints, charlatans, criminals, and every other type of being in the human spectrum.

Remenyi's training serves him well in that he recognizes that poverty has something to do with economics. No doubt that will sound like an amazing idea to someone whose only connection with the issue comes from reading social ethicists or theologians. For many such writers the existence of poverty is an opportunity to expound an ideology that centers on class struggle. Speaking about economic issues, in contrast, seems grubby and uninspiring: Interest rates, demand curves, and $100 loans do not make the heart beat faster. But heart-pounding ideologies have proved to be of no help to poor people in the past and are unlikely to do better in the future.

That is not to say that economic ideas constitute an all-purpose salvation; they also can be panaceas when their virtues are not kept firmly in the place where they can do some good. There is only one kind of situation the CB-IGPs Remenyi describes can remedy, and that is the situation characterized by scarcity of liquidity and investment capital. They have never been able to provide either the cultural strength or political justice that are also necessary for economic prosperity.

Remenyi makes a statement that will appear to some readers to be a quiet truism, but in the context of the actual debates is a blockbuster. He says that projects that actually alleviate poverty do so by "seeking to improve output per person." What's this — the *output* of poor people is to be increased? This will flummox many people associated with the redistribution mentality or with any relief and development program with a "helping-the-poor mentality." It will do so because it is a reversal of the common assumption that you help people by giving *to* them. It says that we help people by getting more *from* them. In a discussion of relieving poverty Remenyi talks about what the poor *provide* rather than what they receive. Although this will seem upside down to redistributors, it is the only sensible way to view the issue. Remenyi's notion and that of many of the NGOs he studied is based on the fact that if we make it possible for poor people to produce goods and services that others desire, they will be able to work their way out of poverty — and provide the means for their friends and neighbors to do the same. People who take seriously the words of the Lord, "It is more blessed to give than to receive" (Acts 20:35), will not be surprised by this.

119

The Spiritual Side and the Legal Setting

K. W. Taylor writes that some NGOs that are explicitly Christian in orientation do not mention that they are in their official reports. Sometimes they do this because they accept government funds and need — or think they need — to downplay their religious motivations and intentions. Taylor says they also exhibit this reticence because their witness, like that of Christ, is more implicit than explicit.[11] But was Jesus all that implicit? He could hardly have been more direct and uncompromising about the presence of the kingdom of God and its relevance for life. There was not much we would want to call "implicit" in a body of teachings full of "hard sayings." Taylor is clearly and justifiably uneasy with attempts to separate the spiritual mission from the physical mission. And he has grave misgivings about Christian mission degenerating into a kind of clone of the Red Cross. He insists that the gospel has had great spiritual impact on the lives of people in the loan programs, and this benefit not only does not show up in the Remenyi study but also does not show up in the official reports of the organizations. I believe he is quite correct about that. These Christian organizations which wear one face for audience A (Christian donors) and another for audience B (government monitors) are likely to reap the bitter fruits of twofacedness.

There will have to be a deepening of spiritual maturity that goes along with CB-IGPs. One reason this is so important is that those who receive help from the NGOs will usually have higher incomes than those they employ, let alone the unemployed, and that introduces a potential thorn on the rosebush: There are ideologies rampant in poor and rich countries alike that cannot abide such inequalities on the grounds that they are evidences of injustice. All envy-based arguments come down to this, and that suggests an issue that I wish Remenyi had done more with. Credit-based programs can do next to nothing to help the poor without cultural and political institutions that will permit them to flourish. If poor people permit envy to dominate their motivations, they will devote more attention to preventing someone else from getting ahead than they will to accomplishing their own necessary tasks. The entrepreneurial spirit can be dampened by envy-produced policies such as confiscatory taxation, price controls, and regulations of various kinds.

11. *Ibid.,* pp. 3f.

In primitive societies it is common for people to refuse to devise a better way to plow their fields because if they then have more than their neighbors, the power of envy will threaten them with despoliation or even death. It does not take much imagination to figure out that this is a picture of a completely static society.[12]

Moreover, the endemic corruption of most poor countries can entangle the most dedicated and energetic entrepreneur in a morass of restrictions and the financial drain of bribery, thus sapping the enterprise. Difficulties of this sort are not amenable to mere institutional tinkering. When I asked the administrator of one NGO if the entrepreneurs to whom he was lending money were operating in accordance with the law, he hesitated for a moment and then reluctantly said, "No." This does not mean that the people were criminals. It means that they were operating in the midst of official lawlessness, where the ordinary activities that people engage in to support themselves are arbitrarily declared to be illegal. What happens to these entrepreneurs when policemen and bureaucrats learn of their activities and demand to be cut in on the gravy? The effect is like slicing the bottom of the CB-IGP purse: The entrepreneurs invest what is left after the officials get "their" share. If the tax system takes much of what is left, what is the future of this system? The recent Russian experience of public indignation at the profits of newly legalized "cooperatives" — "obscene profits" in the parlance of demagogues — has led to punitive taxation that could doom the tender shoot of Russian enterprise.

Remenyi is aware that legal barriers compound the difficulties. He mentions the high cost to the poor of complying with the law in starting and running businesses; consequently few of them do it. In a related matter, he says that taking from the rich to give to the poor is justified — surprising language given the rest of the paper — but only when what is taken away are monopolies and other barriers to enterprise and initiative. The enemy here is "entrenched interests" that profit from the helplessness of poor people by squelching their normal rights to practice economic life. In other words this "taking away" is not the language of envy-driven redistribution that has done so much damage to poor people, but rather the restoration of ordinary justice, with equal protection for all citizens.

12. A masterful account of the ways in which envy destroys economic life is Helmut Schoeck's *Envy: A Theory of Social Behavior*, tr. Michael Glenny and Betty Ross (London: Secker and Warburg, 1969).

121

The caveats I have mentioned here are not intended to detract either from the importance of Remenyi's study, which is considerable, nor of credit-based income generating projects, which are the most hopeful sign yet that institutional efforts to help the poor can succeed. But there are problems with them, some of which are mentioned in the Remenyi study. Others are picked up by Taylor's paper. The Remenyi report had been read by only a few participants of Oxford II when its findings were endorsed by the Declaration; approval came, rather, on the basis of enthusiasm over Remenyi's oral summary and the discussion that followed. Taylor gave a much briefer summary of his paper and I do not believe its cautionary remarks were even considered. Yet without taking into consideration the warnings that Remenyi recognized were necessary, plus Taylor's concerns and others as well, income generating projects can become the same destructive panaceas that foreign aid has been for almost two generations. The fact that these small-scale projects are already becoming something of a buzzword in the foreign aid establishment is not a good sign. That establishment is just as capable of wrecking microprograms as it was of wrecking macroprograms.

Perhaps the best way to avoid such disasters is to pay careful heed to the economic analysis of the Remenyi study along with the spiritual and biblical grounding of Taylor's work. There is much more to be done on both counts. And of course, in the application of these ideas we have barely begun.

PART III

Toward an Ecumenical Consensus

Michael Novak and Derek Cross

A remarkable thing happened near the end of the twentieth century. On large matters of political economy, a group of scholars of evangelical Protestant background, meeting at Oxford University in England, generated a set of judgments quite similar to those pronounced by the Roman Catholic pontiff, Pope John Paul II, in his encyclical letter of May 1, 1992, *Centesimus Annus* ("The Hundredth Year"). Who would have predicted such fraternal consonance?

Both of these documents, the Oxford Declaration and the papal encyclical, are alike in five crucial respects. First, both give their primary allegiance to the gospel, measuring their practical judgments about concrete realities today in the light of biblical teaching. Second, both derive from these teachings certain basic lessons about the dignity of every human person made in the image of God and the liberty and responsibilities inherent in that dignity. On this basis, they give conditional approval to free economies designed to secure the common good and to promote the general welfare within the bounds of law, morality, and justice. Third, both give attention to the Christian imperative to pay special attention to the needs of the world's poor and forgotten ones. In addition, in presenting their arguments and in reaching their conclusions, both documents demonstrate considerable practical wisdom and sophisticated technical judgment. Finally, both documents commend themselves to all persons of goodwill.

All this is a remarkable achievement, and we should pause to reflect on its significance. It would be passing strange if two such documents, both motivated by high Christian seriousness and drawing on similar Christian sources, reached conclusions in which each work was totally opposed to the other. This, of course, could happen. While being faithful to the same Christian inspirations and the same Christian sources, the authors of both documents could have used such radically different understandings of contemporary economic realities that their final practical analysis, however similar in theological provenance, came to radically different concrete conclusions. For it often does happen that Christians of comparable seriousness and devotion do, nonetheless, arrive at radically different analyses of contemporary realities or radically different readings of "the signs of the times." That, in itself, need not be disconcerting. After all, the Christian gospel does not deprive individuals of the responsibility to use their own heads and to apply available intellectual methods in such a way that Christians of goodwill (like other persons of goodwill) might come to different practical judgments. What is quite remarkable is that in this case such an eventuality did not come to pass.

The reason for this may not be difficult to discern. The evident collapse of what even socialists have referred to as "real existing socialism" (in the former Soviet Union and its central European empire) has taught all the world certain lessons. Moreover, it has not only been in the communist nations that socialism has failed to pass the tests of modern life; similarly, the democratic socialist and social democratic parties of western Europe have also come face-to-face with certain intractable economic realities. Chief among these is the recognition of limits to such policies as nationalization, central planning, government spending, and social welfare programs. These are limits that even social democrats and democratic socialists must respect.

Modern economies are made up of free citizens — independent economic agents — and this fact alone brings in its train certain inexorable consequences. To the extent that such free citizens make free market choices, the achievement of the common good depends on billions of free economic transactions. In gaining some intelligence about what free persons want and about how much sweat and effort they are willing to expend in securing these wants, no other technique has been found to work nearly so efficiently, fairly, and intelligently as a market system.

Given such large and sweeping lessons from the experience of our time, the consonance between the Oxford Conference and *Centesimus Annus* is not perhaps too surprising. Let us see how they compare.

Some Comparisons

We are barely into the beginning of the Oxford Declaration on Christian Faith and Economics when in paragraph 6 we read that "The dominion which God gave human beings over creation (Genesis 1:30) does not give them licence to abuse creation." We are further told that "since human beings are created in the image of God for community and not simply as isolated individuals (Genesis 1:28), they are to exercise dominion in a way that is responsible to the needs of the total human family, including future generations." These paragraphs of the Oxford Declaration recall §37 of *Centesimus Annus:*

> In his desire to have and to enjoy rather than to be and to grow, man consumes the resources of the earth and his own life in an excessive and disordered way. At the root of the senseless destruction of the natural environment lies an anthropological error, which unfortunately is widespread in our day. Man, who discovers his capacity to transform and in a certain sense create the world through his own work, forgets that this is always based on God's prior and original gift of the things that are. Man thinks that he can make arbitrary use of the earth, subjecting it without restraint to his will, as though it did not have its own requisites and a prior God-given purpose, which man can indeed develop but must not betray. Instead of carrying out his role as a cooperator with God in the work of creation, man sets himself up in place of God and thus ends up provoking a rebellion on the part of nature, which is more tyrannized than governed by him. . . . In this regard, humanity today must be conscious of its duties and obligations towards future generations.

A few more examples may help to drive home the comparison. We are told in paragraph 8 of the Declaration that "production is not only necessary to sustain life and make it enjoyable; it also provides an opportunity for human beings to express their creativity in the service of others." Compare that passage with §32 of *Centesimus Annus:*

> . . . besides the earth, man's principal resource is *man himself.* His intelligence enables him to discover the earth's productive potential and the many different ways in which human needs can be satisfied. It is his disciplined work in close collaboration with others that makes

127

possible the creation of ever more extensive *working communities* which can be relied upon to transform man's natural and human environments. Important virtues are involved in this process. . . .

Similarly, the very next paragraph in the Declaration (9) tells us that "human creativity is expressed in the designing of tools for celebration and work. Technology helps us meet the basic needs of the world population and to do so in ways which develop the creative potential of individuals and societies." And §32 of *Centesimus Annus* offers us a similar message:

> Whereas at one time the decisive factor of production was the *land* and later capital — understood as a total complex of the instruments of production — today the decisive factor is increasingly *man himself,* that is, his knowledge, especially his scientific knowledge, his capacity for interrelated and compact organization, as well as his ability to perceive the needs of others and to satisfy them.

Again, one might consider the Declaration's paragraph 59, dealing with consumerism, as in the sentence: "The overwhelming consumerism of Western societies is testimony to the fact that the material success of capitalism encourages forces and attitudes that are decidedly non-Christian." This and subsequent paragraphs should be compared with §36 of *Centesimus Annus:*

> If . . . a direct appeal is made to human instincts — while ignoring in various ways the reality of the person as intelligent and free — then consumer attitudes and lifestyles can be created which are objectively improper and often damaging to his physical and spiritual health. Of itself, an economic system does not possess criteria for correctly distinguishing new and higher forms of satisfying human needs from artificial new needs which hinder the formation of a mature personality. Thus a great deal of educational and cultural work is urgently needed, including the education of consumers in the responsible use of their power of choice, the formation of a strong sense of responsibility among producers and among people in the mass media in particular. . . .

Finally, one might compare paragraph 60 of the Declaration — "Such [governmental] structures must respect the principle that significant decisions about local human communities are usually best made at a level of government most directly responsible to the people affected" — with §48 of *Centesimus Annus:*

> . . . the *principle of subsidiarity* must be respected: a community of higher order should not interfere in the internal life of a community of a lower order, depriving the latter of its functions, but rather should support it in case of need and help to coordinate its activity with the activities of the rest of society, always with a view to the common good.

Starting Small Business

These striking correspondences with regard to the principles of social doctrine are not high-sounding platitudes or a self-justifying ideology; they impose obligations on Christians, among them the obligation to seek out concrete measures to alleviate the lot of the poor and, more than that, to break the hold that the culture of poverty has on the poor, by changing institutional structures. We read in paragraph 65 of the Oxford Declaration, for example, that "ethical demands are often ineffective because they are reinforced only by individual conscience" and that "the proclamation of Christian values needs to be accompanied by action to encourage institutional and structural changes. . . ."

Centesimus Annus also insists on the strict linkage of its analysis to the concrete reality of integral human life. Section 48 declares that a state that executed a right to work for all its citizens would necessarily become an oppressive totalitarianism and would crush all free initiative. Having noted this, however, the encyclical does not leap to an abstract affirmation of a society totally given over in all of its dimensions to laissez-faire. The state is concretely related to economic life; the problem is how best to order the elements of human society. Among these elements is, necessarily, a state apparatus with its own political competencies, as well as a zone of free market economy. Since "economic activity is indeed but one sector in a great variety of human activities, and like every other sector, it includes the right to freedom, as well as the duty of making responsible use of freedom" (§32), the encyclical rejects the notion that "the state has no competence in [the economic] domain."

129

Among the proper functions of the state, the encyclical continues, are harmonization and guidance of a developing economy: The state has a duty to sustain business activities by creating conditions that will ensure job opportunities by stimulating those activities where they are lacking or by supporting them in moments of crisis (§48). Thus in the concrete the state neither "withers away" by simply removing itself from the business activities of its citizens nor assumes control over them in a form of economic *dirigisme*. Its role is to enable, facilitate, and support.

Drawing on a similar insight into the role of the state as supporter of economic opportunity, the Oxford Conference has appended to its Declaration on Christian Faith and Economics a "Statement on Income Generation," which is directed to the kind of initiative that might be taken by both state and society to serve the needs of the poor in developing countries. This Statement makes abundantly clear, as does the papal encyclical, that the identity of the true and genuine actors in the economic sphere must ultimately be the poor themselves. "Poverty is not a problem at which one can simply throw money and have it go away," the Statement quotes from a study commissioned by the Conference. Calling for a "new approach" that eschews command economy strategies, the Conference mandates this important requirement: "Poverty alleviation policies must tap the vitality and potential of the private enterprise driven economic goals of the thousands upon thousands of small businesses that employ and service the consumption needs of the poor."

The urgent practical question set by the Statement is how to promote the development of small businesses so that the poor can become entrepreneurs in their own right. As far as government itself is concerned, "enabling" is largely a function of the legislative process. The Statement rightly refers to the "labyrinth of regulations and procedures" that impedes entrepreneurial initiative and thereby marginalizes those whom it banishes into an "illegal sector."

What sort of legislative changes are necessary to dismantle this labyrinth and to regularize the "illegals"? The Statement does not spell out the details. Clearly, new legal structures are a first condition to halt the marginalization of the illegals. Other practical suggestions might also be offered: Fees for the incorporation of small businesses should be no more than a day's wage. The incorporation process should be simplified so that one has to deal with only one registrar of incorporation papers. Incorporation should require no more than a request and exchange of papers by mail. It should take only a couple of weeks to fulfill the necessary procedures.[1]

Another area where legislative reform can make a difference for the poor is the granting of patents and copyrights. Abraham Lincoln pointed to this crucial strategic factor in the building up of Anglo-American civilization:

> The Patent laws . . . began in England in 1624; and, in this country, with the adoption of our Constitution. Before then, any man might instantly use what another had invented; so that the inventor had no special advantage from his own invention. The patent system changed this; secured to the inventor, for a limited time, the exclusive use of his invention; and thereby added the fuel of *interest* to the fire of genius, in the discovery and production of new and useful things. (February 11, 1859, Lecture on Discoveries)

Given the opportunity to profit from their ingenuity and inventions, the poor swiftly become the most creative segment of society. The Oxford Statement also establishes the importance of changing the regulations and procedures of financial institutions so as to extend credit to the poor. Only the ready availability of such credit will enable the poor to acquire property, to create and improve small businesses, to finance further education, and otherwise to expand their economic opportunities.

The Statement contains additional suggestions that merit further study. For example, it proposes that in creditor countries, governments and financial institutions should allow part of the nonserviceable debt of debtor countries to be used to fund credit-based income generation programs. It also proposes that the governments of industrialized countries offer tax credits to individuals for their voluntary contributions to fund income generation programs based on loans to small Third World businesses.

The stress on nongovernmental organizations in the Statement is in accord with discussions of the role of mediating structures in society which have been carried out in the United States and elsewhere.[2] Ac-

---

1. See, e.g., chapter 6 of Michael Novak, *This Hemisphere of Liberty* (rev. ed., Washington: AEI, 1992).

2. Sections 63f. of the Oxford Declaration call to mind, for example, Peter L. Berger and Richard John Neuhaus, *To Empower People: The Role of Mediating Struc-*

131

cording to the Statement, "NGOs must become far more important bridges between the informal and formal sectors in the economy." Deploying a Christian anthropology that affirms the personal subjectivity and dignity of the worker in all its implications, the Statement also encourages the formation of indigenous credit-based institutions. Wisely, its goal is "ultimate independence from foreign donor support."

Seeking new means of ensuring the availability of credit is essential to raising up the poor. It is crucial to invest in the development of "human capital." As *Centesimus Annus* remarks, "In our time in particular there exists another form of ownership which is becoming no less important than land: the possession of know-how, technology and skill. The wealth of industrialized nations is based much more on this kind of ownership than on natural resources" (§32).

Human capital developed through education is today the chief cause of the wealth of nations. The establishment of universal education should be the goal of large private and public investment. Nor should the erection of private school systems, particularly secondary schools and universities, be discouraged. The education dispensed by these institutions will appropriately stress links with the practical arts and sciences necessary for economic development.

The Oxford Declaration concludes with an honest confession of intellectual sin (65): "We acknowledge that all too often we have allowed society to shape our views and actions and have failed to apply scriptural teaching in this crucial area of our lives, and we repent."

The God who made us made us to be creative. We should and do repent for the years when in the paths of moral reflection on economic life we followed, rather than led. Today all the world is beginning to live under the same laws of economics. That fact should not surprise those of us who believe that one God created all things and is the Governor of all.

---

tures in Public Policy (Washington: AEI, 1977), and Michael Novak, ed., *Democracy and Mediating Structures: A Theological Inquiry* (Washington: AEI, 1980).

The Oxford Declaration as a Contribution to the Ecumenical Debate

Rob van Drimmelen

The 1980s have been called the decade of statements, declarations, and pastorals on economic issues. Most of these statements were written in the North, some came from the South and were focused on specific issues such as the debt crisis, and a number were issued by global bodies like the Vatican, the World Council of Churches, and the Oxford Conference on Christian Faith and Economics. This flurry of documents on economic life indicates the importance attached by Christians all over the world to the issues at stake. This is no surprise because economics is about the daily life of people and therefore is an issue about which Christians are concerned. Christian faith cannot make a separation between spiritual and material life. God became incarnate in Jesus Christ to share the human condition with us, and the Lord's Prayer taught to us by Christ is about spiritual life as well as about such material issues as daily bread and forgiving debts. Bread and debts were probably among the most pressing issues for the Israelites, and they are still urgent concerns for many people in the world today. No dichotomy can be made between the spiritual realm and the material realm; if people are starving, that is just as much a religious problem as an economic problem.

Through the centuries, Christians have developed a rich, if diverse tradition of understanding how their faith relates to economic life and how they should practice their obedience in this field. From the early Church Fathers came stern calls to the rich to accept their responsibility regarding the poor and the needy. In the Middle Ages, movements like the Franciscans and Waldensians reminded the established church of the words of the prophets and the teachings of Jesus regarding the urgent need to actively

133

seek practical solutions to alleviate poverty and to do justice. Later, Reformers like Calvin and Luther struggled to discover distinctly Christian ways of handling and regulating human behavior in the economic realm, which was becoming increasingly important in the Europe of their days.

Although the splits within the church which occurred over the centuries seldom arose from economic questions, such questions do affect the ways in which the different traditions that emerged handle such questions. It is the conviction of those in the ecumenical movement that none of our separate traditions or communities is wholly adequate by itself. We are much more likely to be able to discern, voice, and act out the truth and love of God if we can do so in awareness of the whole church with its different manifestations in all parts of the world. Thus all our traditions need to be caught up into dialogues that can ensure mutual challenge and enrichment. The Oxford Declaration is a very welcome and high-quality contribution to this discussion. This brief chapter picks up a few issues mentioned in the Oxford Declaration in an effort to continue the dialogue.

Diversity

Most of the economic pastorals issued in recent years have come from individual churches and have been written in particular national contexts. It has proven to be very difficult to reflect the different social, cultural, and political positions of those living in particular national contexts adequately in these documents and to do justice to them. This problem is amplified when international bodies like the Oxford Conference try to address such complicated issues as economic policies and systems. In a world characterized by enormous historical and cultural differences, it is difficult indeed to go beyond platitudes and to say something that is meaningful in every context.

The issue of culture may serve as an example in this respect. Culture influences the way in which production factors — labor, capital, and land — are used. Culture influences the questions whether slave labor or work on Sunday are acceptable. It also influences the division of labor — for instance, between women and men — as well as what kind of labor should be financially remunerated or not; for example, housekeeping and raising children are not remunerated, but the work of a school teacher is. The logic of capital accumulation that dominates western societies is also not self-evident. There are cultures and societies in which people only produce or collect for their immediate needs, and there are even cultures in which people compete in giving away instead of accumulating (in this context we can also think of the stories told in Acts 2 and 4).

The use of the third production factor, land, is also strongly influenced by culture. In some indigenous cultures, people pray to their gods first before they cut down a tree, almost apologizing for needing the tree or the land. Certain pieces of land may be sacred because ancestors are buried there. This respect for nature, which characterizes most indigenous cultures, contrasts sharply with the disrespect for creation that prevails in modern societies. For such reasons, it is good that the Oxford Declaration reminds us that it is difficult to reach agreement when we come from diverse cultures and subcultures (Preamble). There are no universally valid and globally applicable prescriptions or blueprints for economic policies and systems. By the same token, not one particular political economic system can exclusively be called Christian (paragraphs 54 and 56). Economic policies should take account of the particular cultural and historical contexts in which they are to be applied.

A related issue is that economics always involves value judgments. The economy is not some kind of independent sphere of reality governed by its own neutral and universal laws. Terms like "economic laws" or phrases like "the economy demands that such and such happen" hide the fact that choices have been made by some person or persons on the basis of their value judgments. Part of the task of the testing economic systems and policies according to biblical truth is to discover the underlying value judgments and the "hierarchy of values" on the basis of which the choices are made by the critical actors.

Convergence

Inasmuch as it is necessary to discover the hierarchy of values applied by critical actors in economic life, it is also necessary to identify the criteria and value judgments that we, maybe unconsciously, apply when we test economic policies and systems. Analyses can never be neutral or value-free and therefore it enhances dialogue when we explicitly say through what spectacles we are looking at what is happening around us. An honest and fruitful dialogue requires that we put our cards on the table and clarify from which position we speak.

An effort to this effect is made by the World Council of Churches

(WCC) in its recently adopted study document "Christian Faith and the World Economy Today."[1] This study document was the result of a four-year study that was conducted in a very participatory way. A draft document was discussed by the WCC Central Committee in 1991 and was sent to all WCC member churches for comments. Subsequently the draft was thoroughly revised, and the final text was adopted by the Central Committee in 1992. The WCC identifies four touchstones (called "signposts" in the document) that can serve as criteria and guidelines in every situation, independent of the particular social, historical, and cultural background:

1) The essential goodness of the created order, and the responsibility for it entrusted to humanity;
2) The innate value and freedom of each human being and of all humanity;
3) God's concern, and the covenant in Christ, with all humankind, breaking through whatever barriers we build between us; and
4) The overarching standard for interhuman relationships and behavior: God's justice, to be discovered through a "preferential option for the poor."

Although the Oxford Declaration does not explicitly list its criteria, it is not difficult to distill them from the text. Some may consider this a biased judgment, but I do see a considerable convergence between the views of the Oxford Declaration and those contained in the study document of the WCC:

a) The convictions that God pronounced the whole creation good (paragraph 1) and that we are called to work as God's stewards (2 and 65) are also reflected in the first criterion mentioned in the WCC document.
b) Like the WCC, the Oxford Declaration affirms that justice is basic to Christian perspectives on economic life (Preamble).
c) The Oxford Declaration states that in assessing economic systems from a Christian perspective, we must consider their ability both to generate and distribute wealth and income justly (8). Later in the Declaration this is specified by saying that justice is related

---

1. "Christian Faith and the World Economy Today: A Study Document from the World Council of Churches," WCC Publications, Geneva, 1992.

particularly to what is due to groups such as the poor (38) because God is the defender of the poor (33). These views coincide with those expressed in the fourth criterion used by the WCC.

d) The emphasis on participation and human dignity (40 and 54), the warning that class and status distinctions must not be barriers preventing access to economic and social institutions (55), and the conviction that God created human beings as free moral agents (51) overlap with the second and third criteria of the WCC document.

At another level, both the Oxford Conference and the WCC agree that no particular political or economic system is directly prescribed by Scripture (paragraphs 54 and 56), that work is an ambiguous reality (20) but at the same time central to God's purpose for humanity (25 and 17), that the overwhelming consumerism of western society is decidedly non-Christian (59) and that the obsessive or careless pursuit of material goods is one of the most destructive idolatries in human history (34), that there is a danger that the model of the market will be assumed to be relevant to other areas of life and that people may consequently believe that what the market encourages is therefore best or most true (59), and that there is a need to foster rigorous voluntary associations (63).

Given the basic consensus on these issues, I would like to highlight some topics regarding which further reflection and dialogue are necessary.

Human Nature

Like many economic pastorals, the Oxford Declaration affirms that God is the creator of everything. However, the Declaration qualifies this statement of faith by saying that this does not mean that creation itself is divine (paragraph 1). This is a helpful warning against the danger of romanticizing nature or sacralizing economic laws by considering them as God-given natural laws that cannot and should not be touched by human beings (as the Spanish scholastics did). It is also a warning against a too easy and quick identification of natural disasters with the will of God. Indeed, as the Declaration reminds us (paragraph 3), God created the world and pronounced it "very good" (Gen. 1:31). But God did not say that creation is "perfect." The true meaning of life in all its fullness,

137

as promised to us in John's Gospel (10:10), will only become apparent when God's reign is fully established in a new heaven and a new earth.

The brokenness of creation also affects human beings. We have been given the responsibility and the basic ability to be cocreators with God, but the flip side of this is that we can also reject God's invitation. The prevailing injustices in this world and the violation of God's good creation by human beings are testimonies to the pervasiveness and universality — the "original" character — of sin. Paul struggles with this in his letter to the Romans when he writes that when he wants to do right, only wrong is within his reach and that he feels a prisoner under the law of sin, which controls his conduct (Rom. 7:21ff.). The words of Paul and the recognition that human beings can easily err should humble us when we try to address such complex issues as economics.

Although the awareness of the ability of human beings to sin characterizes all Christian theologies, various traditions put different emphases on this. There are those theological traditions in which people are considered basically good but tempted to do evil, and there are those that start from the assumption that human beings are inclined to do all evil, as stated for example in the Heidelberg Catechism. The economic policies and systems that people try to devise depend on the theological and anthropological assumptions they make about the level of trust that can be put in the nature of human beings. Those who believe in the basic goodness of human nature would be inclined to leave considerable room for individual freedom in the economic realm, but those who have less confidence in the basic inclination of human beings to act justly would rather look for systems of (legal) checks and balances. How we see human nature is therefore an important issue when we address economic issues.

Individual Freedom and Community

The Oxford Declaration points out that human beings are created in the image of God for community and not simply as isolated individuals (paragraph 6). This is a welcome reminder, especially for those who live in societies characterized by growing individualism. At the same time this reminder raises the fundamental question regarding the relationship between individual freedom and community or *koinonia*. The Oxford Declaration rejects both selfish individualism, which neglects human community, and rigid collectivism, which stifles human freedom (paragraph 4).

According to the Declaration, individual self-interest can legitimately be pursued, but only in a context marked by the pursuit of the good for others; these two are complementary (paragraph 22). The question of which political-economic arrangements would provide "a context marked by the pursuit of the good of others" remains unanswered but, for reasons mentioned above, it is wise that the Declaration does not venture to develop blueprints. More thought, however, needs to be given to the statement that the pursuit of individual self-interest is complementary to the pursuit of the common good. The famous World Conference on Church, Community and State, which took place in 1937, also in Oxford, said about this:

> It was thought at one time that the development of this new economic order (capitalism) would not only improve the material conditions of life but would also establish social justice. This expectation was rooted in the belief that a pre-established harmony would so govern the self-interest of individuals as to create the greatest possible harmony in society as a whole. "Each man, seeking his own, would serve the common weal." Today this belief is largely discredited.

These insights contrast with the view of those who believe that the saying "What is good for business is good for America," is not just rhetoric, but that it is true.[2] We can, however, ask ourselves how the statement that the pursuit of individual self-interest is complementary with the pursuit of the common good will be understood by auto workers in the United States, who fear that they will lose their jobs and income (their individual self-interest) because the production of cars might be moved to Mexico to serve the "common good" of the North American Free Trade Zone. We can also ask whether such a statement would convince the sugarcane workers on the Philippine island of Negros, who lost their jobs because soft drink producers replaced cane sugar with substitutes. One community benefits — the soft drink producers (and the consumers by paying lower prices?) — but the other community — the sugarcane workers — is deprived. This illustrates the complexity of the relationships between individuals and communities and among different communities. Whose common good are we talking about? Whereas some democratic countries have gone a long way in the direction of "a context marked by the pursuit of the good of others," the

2. See the article by Timothy Harris in *ESA Advocate*, May 1992.

international economy lacks democratic and efficient institutions and can correctly be described as a jungle where the pursuit of the individual self-interest of the strongest prevails.

In this regard, it is important that the Oxford Declaration points out that biblical values and historical experience call Christians to work for the adequate participation of all people in the decision-making processes on questions that affect their lives (paragraph 54). Along the same line, the Declaration states that significant decisions about local human communities are usually best made at a level of government most directly responsible to the people affected (paragraph 60). International developments, however, go in the opposite direction; the growing internationalization of the world economy tends to shift political and economic decision-making centers away from local levels. We can only understand and address these issues when we engage in serious analyses of power relationships. The economy is always a realm in which power operates in many different ways. There is nothing wrong with power as such, but questions need to be addressed regarding how power is achieved, used, and controlled. Analyses of power structures and identification of the critical actors may reduce feelings of powerlessness regarding complicated issues such as economics.

The questions and issues raised above may illustrate the necessity to continue to study the whole cluster of issues of the relationships between individual freedom and self-interest, participation, community and common good, and power, at the theoretical and theological level as well as at the practical level.

Free Trade

In some quarters, free trade and free enterprise are seen as a panacea to many problems. Some people even go as far as to say that the Bible clearly teaches a free enterprise system of markets.[3] The Oxford Declaration is more nuanced when it states that greater freedom and trade among nations is an important part of reducing poverty worldwide. Few people would contest this, especially when such a statement is put in the context of the growing protectionism in the North (paragraph 43).

3. E.g., James Kennedy in *Christian Perspectives: A Journal of Free Enterprise* 4, no. 2 (Lynchburg, 1991).

But it can be asked whether statements like these should be taken to their logical conclusion to imply that the free movement of people — who follow their individual self-interest — should also be promoted.

Another question is how so-called free trade zones promote community. Surely, trade is free in such zones, but the workers are not free — they are not allowed to organize themselves in trade unions — and their working conditions do not exactly correspond to a dignified human life. What freedom and whose freedom are we talking about? Herman Daly and John Cobb struggle with this issue and propose a system of "balanced trade" as a middle ground between free trade and autarchy.[4]

Yet another question regards the relationship between free trade and the environment. Should restrictions be put on free trade, for example, in regard to hazardous wastes or endangered species, in order to protect the environment? How can we deal with the fact that deteriorating terms of trade for the Two-Thirds World stimulates wasteful and environmentally destructive ways of production and consumption? What about free trade in drugs (cocaine, opium, and the like), tobacco, arms? On the basis of what value judgments and analyses do we arrive at the conclusion that trade in certain products should be free or should not? Questions like these illustrate that the statement that greater freedom and trade among nations is desirable has to be qualified. More thought needs to be given to how freer trade affects different communities.

Connected with these questions is the issue of economic growth. It is surprising that nowhere does the Oxford Declaration ask whether there are limits to economic growth. The Declaration does refer to ecological destruction in relation to human greed (paragraph 3), it warns against overwhelming consumerism (59), and it points to our task to help sustain creation (6). It also has some very good things to say about the role of technology (9-13), but nowhere is the fundamental question asked whether, from an ecological point of view, there are limits to uncontrolled economic growth. Nevertheless, this is a very important issue, as was illustrated again during the UN Conference on Environment and Development, which was held in Rio de Janeiro in 1992. Could creation sustain a situation in which the world as a whole would enjoy the same living standards, levels of production and consumption, as presently prevailing for the majority of those living in the rich

---

4. *For the Common Good: Redirecting the Economy Toward Community, the Environment and a Sustainable Future* (Boston: Beacon, 1989).

countries? Will technological developments be adequate in limiting environmental destruction to secure sustainable development?

The WCC study document emphasizes that there are plenty of areas in this world still needing a level of production that would provide employment and income in order to enable a dignified human life for all. For those areas, economic growth remains absolutely necessary. Indeed, the production of goods can be a blessing, as the word "good" in fact suggests. But to claim and possess more and more goods does not necessarily lead to greater happiness for those who already enjoy high standards of living. Ever-increasing production and consumption can, paradoxically, lead to increasing scarcity rather than wealth and happiness. Goods like clean air, clean water, stillness, and time are becoming more and more scarce. Unpriced scarcity of so-called non-economic goods is on the increase and while it seems that, through increased production, we have been moving from scarcity to greater wealth, we are really moving in the opposite direction. According to economist Bob Goudzwaard,[5] the emergence of generalized scarcity is due to the reality that human needs and desires have increased faster than has our ability to meet them. When this occurs, and when we assume that human needs are virtually limitless, then scarcity increases, regardless of the current level of material prosperity. Many seem to have lost the perception of *enough.* There are both material and spiritual limits to economic growth.

Just as humanity has more or less developed a sense of a required minimum of consumption to ensure a decent life, so we should be considering where the maximum limits may lie and how those might be implemented, before excess leads to ruin. The maxims "live more simply so that others may simply live" and "nobody should add to their affluence until everybody has their essentials" cannot be easily applied under the conditions we inherit today, but they do remain true and urgent. The WCC Assembly in Canberra in 1991 reminded us that "growth for growth's sake is the strategy of the cancer cell." Therefore, questions like what is to be produced, under what conditions, by whom, for whom, and at what costs need to be high on our agenda.[6]

5. "Economics and Ethics — Starting Point or Afterthought?" *The Catalyst* (Canada), February 1992.

6. See also *Sustainable Growth — A Contradiction in Terms? Economy, Ecology and Ethics after the Earth Summit* (Geneva: Visser t' Hooft Foundation).

Private and Public Sector

After the collapse of the centrally planned economic systems in Central and Eastern Europe, there is a tendency to be triumphalistic about the victory of the free market systems and to see this as the end of history. Fortunately, the Oxford Declaration does not fall into this trap. The "victorious" system also has many deficiencies and some of them are mentioned in the Declaration. Today, the basic challenge is knowing how political freedom can be combined with enough freedom in the economic realm while securing effective and efficient social security networks. The real debate is not about whether a choice has to be made between centrally planned and laissez-faire economic systems. Neither is the issue whether economic decisions should be made exclusively by the state or by the market and the private sector. Both of them have a role to play regarding economic matters. In each situation it is important to decide how they combine to bring about a just, participatory, and sustainable order. The answers to many of these problems and issues will have to be found through participatory political processes, and the Oxford Declaration correctly points to the crucial role that has to be played in this respect by civil society (paragraph 63).

The Statement on Income Generation Programmes among the Poor in Developing Countries puts a welcome emphasis on the need to increase substantially the poor's access to credit and other development resources through credit-based income generation programs. Grants to poor people and vulnerable groups will probably always be necessary but, wherever possible, ways should be found for the poor to help themselves. In general this is more effective and also more respectful of human dignity. Credit-based programs are an important example in this respect. Therefore, the Statement calls for a new approach, one that respects and makes use of the atomistic nature of competition in the survival economy of the poor.

This statement raises a basic question: Is the guiding motivation competition or cooperation? Those who trust in the market are relying on competition as a positive force, and they will readily regard others as naive for expecting cooperation to work in a sinful and broken world. Those who have had encouraging experiences of cooperation will insist that competition is bound to prove harmful if it is allowed more than a limited place. Again, this question relates to how we see human nature. In part this is a theological debate between those who trust in the "already" of the salvation offered in Christ and want to work this out

143

in the practice of cooperation and those who believe that the achievement of salvation is "yet to come" and that meanwhile human behavior must take the fallenness of humanity fully into account.

According to the earlier mentioned WCC study document, both have a point; Christians can only go on pilgrimage through this world as those who are seeking to be both as "wise as serpents" (fully aware of sin and its power) and as "harmless as doves" (always expecting and welcoming self-giving love). In economic practice, this probably means allowing for both: competition in appropriate domains, always controlled against trickery and manipulation, alongside cooperative arrangements for other domains, and both in frameworks of democratic accountability.

A weakness of the Statement is that it focuses all its attention on the ways in which the state ignores and even hinders microenterprises and the informal sector. While this is certainly true (many examples of this can be given), the private sector and international economic structures can also be very destructive for microenterprises (e.g., after Unilever entered the soap market in Kenya, the small local soap industries were virtually destroyed). Therefore, the Statement needs to be read alongside the Oxford Declaration, which does recognize these problems, for example, where it points to transnational corporations, which can wield enormous influence on some economies (paragraph 57), where it refers to powerful nations and corporations that are regularly tempted to use technology to dominate the weak for their own narrow self-interest (9), and where it recognizes the need for a radical restructuring both of national economic policies and international economic relations (42).

It is a pity that nowhere in the Statement on Income Generation Programmes among the Poor is reference made to important initiatives that have already been taken in this field by churches and church-related organizations. The Statement can easily give the impression that the importance of this issue has only just been discovered by churches and Christians. However, already in the 1940s the WCC established the Ecumenical Church Loan Fund (ECLOF), which basically works with revolving funds, and in the early 1970s the WCC took the initiative to establish the Ecumenical Development Cooperative Society (EDCS). The primary objectives of the EDCS are:

1) to work with poor people in their efforts for self-reliance through job and wealth creation by providing loans, guaranties, or investment capital;

2) to be a model for a more just economic order, demonstrating that an enterprise can operate on Christian principles, helping poor people, and yet be a viable business; and

3) to provide an instrument for the churches to share in a more just distribution of wealth by using their capital in economic development among the poor.

Through the EDCS, churches and Christians are challenged to put their money where their mouth is by investing (part of) their investment capital and savings in this corporation. While accepting a lower financial return than could be obtained through "normal" investments, a high social return is achieved. Shareholders in the EDCS have one vote independent of the number of shares they hold, thereby expressing the will to share decision-making power. The share capital stands at around US$62,000,000, and over the years, the EDCS has been instrumental in helping to improve the economic status of some 200,000 poor people through enterprises owned, managed, and worked in by them. Granted, this is a drop in the bucket considering the enormous needs that exist, but as a sign of hope, initiatives such as these are important enough to be mentioned in this context.

At first sight, it may be surprising that a document like the Statement on Income Generation Programmes among the Poor mentions the need for more work to be done on missiological questions. However, this is not so strange as it may look. For those who have eyes to see, it is clear that, in economic life, we are surrounded by a whole pantheon of false gods and idols who are worshiped and who ask tremendous sacrifices. If mission is about inviting people to turn away from idols and turn to the living God, economic life is a vast mission field. But this mission field includes churches, which are too often part and parcel of existing structures. According to the Roman Catholic Bishops of the United States, the political economy is one of the chief areas where we live out our faith. The Oxford Declaration is a strong call to all of us to acknowledge this and to live out our Christian faith in the economic realm in a way that the tree is recognized by its fruits, so that the world may believe.

What Does the Lord Require?
Three Statements on Christian Faith
and Economic Life

Donald Hay

The collapse of communism in Eastern Europe and the former Soviet Union, and the consequent abandonment of the policies and institutions of centralized economic planning in favor of market-based systems has rewritten, at least in part, the agenda that has to be addressed by Christian ethics for economic life. Other parts of the agenda remain the same, notably international disparities in income and the impact of international economic policies, but even there the discrediting of economic planning has changed the emphasis of the discussion. Market "solutions" are to the fore, and the only issues are how these solutions are to be applied and the design of appropriate institutional mechanisms.

It is therefore particularly opportune that the last three years have seen the production of major statements on economic issues by Christian bodies representing three strands in theology and ethics. The first such statement was the encyclical *Centesimus Annus,* promulgated by Pope John Paul II in 1991, which expounds official Roman Catholic teaching. The second was the World Council of Churches (WCC) study document Economy as a Matter of Faith, which reflects liberal Protestant theological ethics. The third is the Oxford Declaration on Christian Faith and Economics, which is informed by an evangelical perspective corresponding to the doctrinal stance of the Lausanne Covenant.

The formal status of these three documents is very different. The Oxford Declaration has no more authority in evangelical circles than that of the signatories. It is the result of a private initiative by the Oxford Centre for Mission Studies. The participants were invited; they are not representatives of other bodies, though a great effort was made to include all shades of opinion within evangelicalism. One wonders why the initiative had to be private: Perhaps the Lausanne Committee feels that such discussions are too "political," or just not central to their concerns.

The WCC document was the work of an advisory group on economic issues within the Council. It was produced after the 1991 Canberra Assembly in response to some of the concerns expressed by that Assembly. While it reflected the consensus within the WCC secretariat, it came to be replaced by a statement that, though initially based on the study document, was substantially different. This final statement was adopted by the WCC Central Committee in 1992.

Centesimus Annus is a very different document: As a papal encyclical it carries all the authority of the official teaching of the Roman Catholic Church. While no doubt many Catholic theologians and ethicists played a part in the research and drafting, it was issued in the name of Pope John Paul, and he had a major influence on the document, both in its general stance and in its detailed statements.

It is convenient to compare and contrast these three documents under four headings: method, context, content, and application. These four areas enable us to identify the distinctiveness of each and their points of agreement.

Method

The Oxford Declaration

Differences of ethical method reflect differing theological views of the basis for the authority of Christian ethical statements. The fundamental problem for Christian economic ethics is how to make the transition from basic doctrinal or ethical insights to the complex world of economic phenomena. Different solutions to that problem almost certainly reflect differences about authority in the church. The Oxford Declaration is explicit on this question: ". . . Scripture, the word of the living and true God, is our supreme authority in all matters of faith and conduct. Hence we turn to Scripture as our reliable guide . . ." (Preamble). The Declaration illustrates the method: Scriptural teaching concerning economic life is summarized under headings such as "Creation and Stewardship" and "Work and Leisure." There is no discussion

147

of the hermeneutical problems involved in using the biblical materials in this way, and no justification of the method is attempted. But the summaries are much more than a listing of texts: Each is a reasoned statement of ethical principles that are claimed to underlie the texts. The applications of these principles follows within each section of the Declaration. The model of application is a critique of a particular aspect of economic life followed (sometimes) by policy proposal, though the latter is seldom fully worked out.

The WCC Study Document

The WCC document begins with individual stories of economic hardship. It continues with a major section on "Today's economic context: the failure of old systems." Throughout the document there are constant reminders that economic ethics must be "contextualized" — that is, they must be developed in the context of actual problems and cultures and not considered as an abstract system of thought. Having described the context, a section follows with "Some fundamental convictions on economic life." These convictions are drawn from theological affirmations about human life and its significance. Some are quite general, for instance, the idea that human beings are to be understood as individuals in community, while others are much more specific, for instance, the Jubilee Principle. There is no discussion of the authority of these "convictions" as a tool for ethical reflection. Nor is there any attempt to systematize them into a set of ethical principles: They are only a listing of points.

In the next section of the document, these convictions are allowed to interact, in a fairly unrigorous manner, with the contemporary context to generate a set of "Goals and visions for economic life." These are, as might be expected, rather more specific than the "convictions," but they are once again presented as a shopping list of desiderata rather than as a coherent statement about economic life or a fully developed theological ethic. From these goals and visions, a section entitled "The need for economic policies" returns to some of the contemporary issues with which the paper began and outlines the policy questions, without, however, detailing appropriate policy responses. Doubts are expressed as to whether it is the task of the church to provide more detailed policy prescriptions.

One criticism of the method of the WCC study document is that the discussion is loosely structured, both within and between sections. The main drift of the argument is easy to follow, but the detailed development from "fundamental convictions" to "goals and visions" to "the need for policies" is not given. Perhaps this weakness arises from the authors' conviction that economic ethics must be developed for concrete problems, and not in the abstract.

Centesimus Annus

The papal encyclical carries the full authority of the Roman Catholic Church by virtue of the authority ceded to St. Peter and his successors in the See of Rome. The 100th anniversary referred to in the title of the encyclical is that of the encyclical *Rerum Novarum,* promulgated by Pope Leo in 1891. *Centesimus Annus* describes *Rerum Novarum* as seminal in the development of the Church's social teaching or "social magisterium." Detailed references in the document are largely to other encyclicals or statements by the Church or popes.

The argument of the encyclical is clear and uncompromising. The starting point is essentially the Christian doctrine of the human person, though reference is made at appropriate points to the doctrine of creation. From the doctrine of humanity, various ethical principles are derived, for example, the rights of workers, the right to private property, the principle of solidarity, and the principle of human freedom (and hence only limited government). These principles are then used to evaluate economic life and to propose general economic policies to put right the wrongs that have been identified. However, this application is not abstract or general: Rather it is set in the context of a commentary on recent economic and political events.

In comparison with the other two documents, the encyclical scores in presenting both an analysis of contemporary events and problems (so it is fully contextualized), and a well-argued theological ethic for economic life. The authoritative basis of the document is very evident, compared to the much more tentative exploration in the WCC study document. For non–Roman Catholic readers there may, of course, be a question mark over the presumed authority of papal statements, even though there may be much in the content with which one could agree. But without the resort to papal authority, the methodological issues in the development of Christian social ethics emerge once again. The same issues are likely to remain an area for debate for some time to come.

Context

Centesimus Annus

The contexts in which the three documents were produced affected their content and objectives. This is most marked in the case of *Centesimus Annus*. The encyclical claims that the downfall of communism in Eastern Europe is a triumphant vindication of the critique of socialism developed by Pope Leo in *Rerum Novarum*. It goes on to argue, no doubt with the Polish example in mind, that Roman Catholic social teaching and the faithful witness of the church to that teaching was instrumental in bringing about the demise of socialism, though it acknowledges that this claim and the analysis that supports it are not authoritative in the same sense as the "social magisterium."

The encyclical recalls that *Rerum Novarum* was written as an analysis of "the worker question," the conflict between capital and labor that emerged in the late nineteenth century, notably the problems of low wages, poor working conditions, and unemployment that had come to characterize the industrial economies. The socialist solution to these problems was class struggle, the abolition of private property, and the rule of the proletariat. The contribution of *Rerum Novarum* was to establish that the Roman Catholic Church had a role in addressing issues of political economy, to begin to develop an appropriate ethic for economic life based on Christian doctrines, and to use this ethic to counter the prescriptions of the socialists.

In *Rerum Novarum* Pope Leo developed key principles from Christian doctrine. He affirmed the fundamental rights of workers at their work, based on the dignity of human beings made in the image of God. These rights included the right of free association in trade unions, which were seen as an instrument for exercising countervailing power to the capitalists, to improve the conditions of the working class, and the right to Sunday rest for recreation and worship. To these workers' rights the pope added the right to private property, in contradiction of socialist claims. This right was not, however, to be considered absolute: Property is held not only for one's own benefit but for the benefit of one's neighbors as well.

150

Centesimus Annus claims that the Church's teachings concerning these rights were instrumental in enabling trade unions to secure improved conditions and wages for their workers at least in Western Europe, which prompted other reforms — social security systems, pensions, health care — which have been widely introduced during the twentieth century in industrial economies. The critique in *Rerum Novarum* identified socialism's erroneous anthropology as its key defect. The atheism and rationalism of socialists denied the Christian doctrine of humankind, and therefore the fundamental dignity and worth of each person. Instead, the person only exists in relation to the class of which he or she is a member. This makes irrelevant the decisions of the individual, subordinating him or her to the interests of his or her class. Private property is an irrelevance in this thinking, and in the hands of the bourgeoisie it is a barrier to economic development and improvement for the workers. To improve the conditions of the workers, class struggle and the violent dispossession of the capitalists are essential. By contrast, Roman Catholic teaching seeks to promote social and economic change through nonviolent protest, based on fundamental doctrines of human dignity and wealth, seeking to persuade and challenge those with responsibility for economic and social ills, but not seeking to destroy or dispossess them.

The WCC Study Document

The WCC document has a very different context. Over the years the WCC analysis of economic life has been sympathetic to socialist solutions. The discrediting of socialist analysis and the demise of socialist planned systems must therefore be something of an embarrassment to the authors of the document. The strategy of the document is therefore to engage in a searching critique of market systems, while acknowledging that solutions to economic problems will in future involve adaptation of markets rather than replacement of them by planning. The document makes no reference to class, to struggle, or to other Marxist categories: The nearest it gets is a discussion of "empowerment ministries," organizing the poor and oppressed to exercise countervailing power against their oppressors. The study document is much more explicitly theological and biblical than previous WCC documents: This is a welcome development in WCC thinking on these issues, and holds out the promise of more explicitly Christian analyses in the future.

151

DONALD HAY

The Oxford Declaration

The context of the Oxford Declaration is that of considerable disagreement and debate within evangelical churches on issues of economics and politics. Evangelical writers on economic life have taken a variety of positions that run the entire gamut from right-wing advocates of markets and economic freedom to left-wing analyses that draw at least some inspiration from socialist theory and practice. This diversity is, of course, something of an embarrassment given that all those involved claim the authority of Scripture for the positions that they hold and advocate. The objective of the study process and of the Conference that produced the Declaration was therefore to see whether any degree of consensus could be achieved among sharply divergent views.

Some of the participants in the process were initially skeptical about what could be achieved, and were surprised and greatly encouraged by the extent to which views converged. Convergence can be achieved in different ways: One is to go for a "lowest common denominator" type of statement, which is either minimal in content or so restricted in its range that "agreement" camouflages much greater disagreements on matters that are not included in the document. That does not, however, appear to be the case with the Oxford Declaration, at least in respect of its basic scriptural convictions concerning economic life. Where it is much less specific is in the analysis of particular economic issues and in the remedies that should be sought. It is at that level that differences are likely to be most acute. However, that should not necessarily be seen as unhealthy. While Christians must surely agree that unemployment, for example, is a social evil, there seems to be every reason why they might disagree on appropriate remedies. Economic analysis is by no means unanimous on either the causes of unemployment or the effects of different policies. To seek to identify a "Christian" economic policy for unemployment is probably an unrewarding activity.

Content

In comparing the content of the three documents we may focus separately on what they have to say about Christian convictions concerning economic life, what they identify as the major economic policy issues

152

to be addressed, and how they perceive the role of the state and of the churches in the pursuit of economic justice.

Economic Life

On Christian principles for economic life there is a considerable degree of convergence despite the diversity of theological positions represented in these three documents. First, the theological themes of creation and stewardship are present in all three as a basis for economic life, as part of the human calling, and as a warning not to destroy the created order, which belongs to God and for which we are responsible stewards.

Second, all three documents place a major emphasis on the theology of the nature of humankind. Work is part of the vocation of each person, the purpose of work being primarily, but not exclusively, to provide for human needs. There is therefore a basic right to work, working conditions should respect human dignity, and remuneration for work should be sufficient to support a worker and his or her dependents. The organization of work should be seen as expressing community between those who work in a particular place: In the words of the encyclical, business should be a community of persons rather than a community of capital goods. Moreover, the right to work is balanced by a right to rest and recreation, linked especially in *Centesimus Annus* to the right to set aside Sunday for Christian worship.

Third, all three documents give prominence to the "preferential option for the poor," which is described as a major biblical theme. One aspect is purely economic: Those who cannot provide for themselves through productive work are to be given sustenance and support by the community in which they live. Another aspect is that the weak and disadvantaged need particular protection to see that they are not oppressed, that their rights are protected and they are given every encouragement to be involved in community life.

Furthermore, the consequence of sinful human nature for economic life is a common theme: Every area of economic life — our stewardship of the creation, the nature of our work, the position of the weak and disadvantaged — is seen to be distorted by sin, with destruction of the environment, alienation at work, and oppression of the poor being the consequences of sin.

Despite the wide area of agreement, there are also some notable differences of emphasis. For example, the WCC study document makes much of the point that responsible stewardship requires that those who wield economic power need to be made accountable, not just to God, but also to their community. This statement also gives greater emphasis to *koinonia* as a principle for all human life, including economic life; and it alone makes use of the biblical concept of the Jubilee. The Oxford Declaration spells out the doctrine of stewardship as a positive mandate to use human creativity and initiative to create wealth, but warns that technology should be subordinated to human ends and not be allowed to develop autonomously without careful consideration of its human and other consequences. *Centesimus Annus* has a number of distinctive emphases. There is, for example, much discussion of the family as basic to human flourishing (linked to the familiar Roman Catholic positions of birth control and abortion). Private property is upheld and defended, following the arguments of *Rerum Novarum,* though subject to the constraint that material goods and resources are to be used for the good of all and not selfishly. A further distinct emphasis is on the role of human knowledge and acquired skills, and on the division (or coopera-tion) of labor in the productive process.

Economic Policy Issues

Turning next to issues, there is considerable agreement among the documents as to the major areas of economic life that need to be addressed. Although market economies are judged to be relatively more effective in ensuring that resources are well used, there is considerable concern expressed about the ideology and culture of markets. Thus there are warnings against treating the market as an idol that can solve all society's problems and against the culture of selfishness and consumer-ism that it can promote. Alienation at work is perceived to be a problem arising from the treatment of labor as just an input to production, failing to respect human dignity and the human sense of vocation. Unemploy-ment is condemned as a grave social evil. The continued existence of poverty alongside considerable affluence both within countries and between countries is highlighted as a key issue for the churches. There is some difference of emphasis in the definition of poverty: *Centesimus Annus* gives greater weight to absolute poverty (meeting the basic needs of the family unit), whereas the Oxford Declaration and the WCC document define poverty in more relative terms as a standard of life that effectively precludes participation in the full life of the community. All the documents underline the problem of Third-World debt and give a high priority to the search for solutions. Finally, all three stress the impending world environmental crisis and urge that action be taken before the damage to the ecosystem becomes irremediable.

Apart from these common concerns there are some differences of focus. *Centesimus Annus* shows much more interest in social institutions and their structures — the family, the business firm, and intermediate associations such as trade unions and voluntary organizations — in the context of economic life. The WCC document gives prominence to the arms race and the international trade in arms. It also stresses, along with the Oxford Declaration, that those who exercise economic power (e.g., in transnational corporations) must be made accountable for their actions to other than their shareholders. The Oxford Declaration includes inflation, drug trafficking, discrimination, and the relative neglect of the informal sector in developing countries as other major policy issues.

The agenda to be addressed is full of very complex issues. None of the documents is able to progress beyond identifying the ethical problems and perhaps a few hints as to where solutions should be sought. Holding back from detailed analysis and the pursuit of solutions may, of course, be appropriate strategy for the churches. The WCC document in particular eschews the identification of specific policy recommendations on the grounds that each society should be allowed to seek solutions that are appropriate to its own culture and traditions.

The Role of the State

But who is to act? The WCC study document does not address this question directly, but evidently accepts that the solution of economic problems is a responsibility of government. Within one country, government should be fully accountable to its citizens for the policies that it promotes. Internationally, the document proposes greater powers for bodies like the United Nations, but says that such bodies should be less dominated by the rich and powerful nations and more responsive to the needs of poorer countries. The WCC document presupposes, and therefore presumably approves of, powerful, interventionist governments. The Oxford Declaration includes a whole section devoted to "Freedom,

Government, and Economics," probably because this has been a major area of disagreement within evangelicalism. [The Declaration explores a Christian concept of human rights based on the doctrine of persons made in the image of God, affirms democratic government that respects those rights, and warns against concentrations of economic power that are not fully accountable.]

Centesimus Annus underlines the responsibilities of government in a number of areas: provision of the juridical framework for economic activity, assurance of appropriate conditions at work and adequate wages, actions to combat unemployment, welfare provisions at an adequate level, and measures to support family life. However, given that the document is rejoicing in the downfall of communist totalitarian regimes, there is no enthusiasm for powerful, interventionist governments. It is acknowledged that intervention in markets will sometimes be necessary, but this should be kept to a minimum. The principle of subsidiarity is affirmed: That is, action should be decentralized as far as possible. No level of government should take responsibility for a matter that can be effectively dealt with by a lower level of government, or indeed by some other institution ("intermediate association"), including the family or the churches. A similar point is made by the Oxford Declaration with its reference to "mediating structures" that are neither public nor private (in the individualistic sense). [While all three documents are agreed that government should be democratically accountable, there is a definite difference of view as to how much intervention in economic life is appropriate. The WCC document is probably the most, and *Centesimus Annus* the least, approving of intervention.]

The Role of the Churches

The WCC document has a lengthy concluding section detailing how it believes that churches should respond to economic issues. Obviously it urges that churches should have a "commitment to dealing with economic issues from a faith perspective," and the statement is seen as a contribution to that process. Furthermore, it urges that Christians and churches should undertake a searching examination of their own lifestyles, priorities, structures, and involvement, direct or indirect, in economic life in the light of the Christian vision of economic justice. Unless the church can reform itself in the light of Christian teaching, then it has no right to address the secular authorities. Beyond that, the church should engage in "transformational ministries." These involve taking a prophetic stance in identifying economic injustice, offering alternative visions for economic life, engaging in advocacy on particular issues and in "empowerment" ministries, organizing the poor and the oppressed to exercise countervailing power to the forces that are oppressing them. These ministries are not lightly advocated: Indeed they are described as "formidable undertakings" for the churches.

Centesimus Annus, by contrast, says very little about the mechanisms by which the Roman Catholic Church seeks to influence economic policy. It notes that *Rerum Novarum* established that the Church had a role in addressing society's problems. It claims that *Rerum Novarum* was instrumental in reforms to improve the conditions of workers in the industrial economies in the twentieth century and that the role of the Church was decisive in the overthrow of communism in Eastern Europe. It clearly assumes that what the new encyclical has to say will be taken seriously not only within the Roman Catholic Church but by a wider audience. This confidence probably reflects the knowledge that the Roman Catholic Church does have an influential presence in many areas of political and economic life. Part of this presence is officially recognized representation, part is through discreet but well-organized pressure groups, and part is the fact that Roman Catholics hold key positions in secular institutions and are prepared to allow the teaching of the Church to influence their policy decisions. This influential presence should not be viewed as a "conspiracy," as some ultra-Protestant groups assert. Rather it reflects a success in promoting the social teaching of the Roman Catholic Church, which other Christian groups would like to emulate. One interesting question is how the Roman Catholic Church would respond to the WCC concept of "empowerment" ministries. Reading the definition of such ministries in the WCC document, one is immediately struck by the parallel with the role of the Roman Catholic Church in promoting the cause of the Solidarity trade union in Poland. Why then is the Vatican so suspicious of the empowerment ministries of the base communities in Latin America, especially those in Brazil, given this statement in *Centesimus Annus:* "Love for others, and in

157

the first place love for the poor . . . , is made concrete in the promotion of justice"?

The Oxford Declaration has no program for action by the churches. It merely states: "We will therefore endeavor to seek every opportunity to work for the implementation of the principles outlined in this Declaration. . . ." This probably reflects the fact that the Declaration was essentially a private initiative without formal recognition by any of the evangelical denominations. In principle, at least, the WCC document can be disseminated via the member churches (though one doubts whether this mechanism is particularly effective). That option is not available to the Oxford Declaration, and it is far from obvious where the process can go next. Who is going to read it, study it, and promote it? Roman Catholics have to take note of encyclicals: There is no parallel obligation on evangelicals to take the Oxford Declaration seriously.

What can we learn from these three documents? First, they illustrate very clearly the continuing divergence of Roman Catholic, liberal Protestant, and evangelical traditions on the source and authority of Christian social ethics. A caricature is that they represent respectively the authority of the traditions of the church, the primacy of reason, and the authority of Scripture. That is a simplification: Tradition, reason, and Scripture are present in all three documents. But the caricature does effectively characterize the nature of the documents. One consequence is that *Centesimus Annus* and the Oxford Declaration are more rigorously developed and argued than the WCC document. A clear and authoritative basis for social ethics permits a more systematic exposition.

Second, the three documents demonstrate a considerable degree of agreement on what might be termed Christian principles for economic life. But the encyclical pays more attention to social and economic institutions than do the other two, and is therefore more balanced in its approach. Third, there is also considerable agreement on the economic and political issues to be addressed by the churches in the aftermath of the collapse of communist planned economies. Fourth, there is agreement that governments have to be involved in economic policy, and that they should be democratically accountable for their decisions. There seems to be less agreement on how much intervention in economic life is appropriate. Where international economic issues are concerned, there is a willingness to give more power to international agencies to regulate and to redress injustices. Fifth, there is agreement that economic and political life is a legitimate (and indeed necessary) sphere of involvement for the churches, though only the WCC document spells out how this involvement might be implemented.

There is a great disparity in the quality of these documents. *Centesimus Annus* stands out as being better researched, better argued, and better written than the other two. The contemporary situation is acutely observed and analyzed. There is the appeal to a tradition or social ethic that has been vindicated by the fall of communism, and there is an implicit assumption that when the Roman Catholic Church speaks things will actually happen (as it is claimed they have in the past). One wonders whether liberal Protestants or evangelicals will ever be able to deal with these issues with such apparent authority and sophistication. But that raises the question whether one would wish them to have that ability.

Those who respond in the affirmative might use the analogy of agreed doctrinal or confessional statements. If, for example, evangelicals can draw up agreed statements of faith such as the Lausanne Covenant, is it not appropriate to seek similar agreement on economic issues and on how such issues might be dealt with, even if it may take many more years of study and discussion to arrive at a common mind? The obvious reply is that doctrinal statements are based on primary truths about God, revealed in Scripture, whereas Christian approaches to political and economic questions have always been considered secondary and derivative. For that response to be countered, it has to be shown that the distinction between doctrinal beliefs and economic issues is not scriptural.

Another question is the use to which agreed statements might be put. Agreement on doctrinal issues clearly affects intercommunion among churches and commitments to work together in evangelism and mission. It seems implausible that an agreement on Christian views of economic issues would be similarly used! It might therefore be more appropriate to view the Oxford Declaration as a summing up of the point that evangelicals have reached in their analysis of Christian ethics for economic life. But, in that case why is there so much emphasis on an *agreed* statement, which one suspects may be interpreted quite differently by different participants in the process? It might have been more helpful, at least to those of us evangelicals who are seeking to contribute to the discussion, to identify areas of agreement and disagreement as a basis for further work. Given its provenance, that is the most likely use to which the Declaration will be put.

Stewardship in the Nineties: Two Views

Lawrence Adams and Fredrick Jones

B efore the celebration of Earth Day in spring 1990 gave a crescendo to renewed environmental consciousness, Christians from various traditions were working toward updated understandings of what it means to be stewards of the earth. Two attempts to forge fresh statements about the relationship between humans and the rest of creation touch sensitive political and economic matters. Yet they each represent major efforts, from quite different starting points, to relate theology to the question of human use of the material world.

The Justice, Peace, and the Integrity of Creation (JPIC) convocation organized by the World Council of Churches (WCC) was guided by the need in the ecumenical world to make a radical departure from existing modes of Christian ethics because of its sense that a human-fabricated crisis is leading to the brink of economic and ecological apocalypse. The Oxford Declaration on Christian Faith and Economics, while sensing urgency, seems driven more by a new confidence in the ability of Christians to connect the recent "lessons" of current events to theological orthodoxy. It is based on a renewed hope about the possibility of responsible Christian action in the world.

Of course, no matter what the issue, no matter how small the group, consensus can be a difficult thing to achieve. Since it is so unusual, it is enlightening to examine both the process of achieving consensus and the substance of consensual agreements themselves.

Background: The Need for New Frameworks

The WCC gathered representatives from a variety of churches and non-Christian traditions from around the world in Seoul, South Korea, in March 1990 with the intent of affirming JPIC as a new and comprehensive approach to understanding the world and the God who made it. The resulting document aims at redefining the orthodox meaning of the gospel. From this broad framework, those entering into its ecumenical affirmations are required to leap to some specific and urgent public policy positions.

The discussions surrounding the Oxford Declaration were, by comparison, the result of a less ambitious undertaking, and few participants probably thought anything so comprehensive would come of it. Many attributed the success in drafting a document that virtually every participant could sign to the new context of international life — including the more desperate and powerless condition of impoverished peoples and the extreme failure of certain policy structures (primarily of socialism) to do anything but make things worse. The relaxing of superpower tensions perhaps freed everyone to take a fresh look at these now unrefutable realities, and the repudiation of communist governments in Europe contributed to a renewed appreciation of human freedom.

To the degree that it is fair to generalize and set up simple contrasts, it can be said that the JPIC group went to Seoul with a great deal of theological diversity and sociopolitical unity, while the Oxford group went to London with greater sociopolitical diversity and more theological unity. This is manifest in the two documents: JPIC is eclectic and inclusive in theological terms, but specific and single-minded when analyzing the world's economic and ecological conditions and prescribing policies. Oxford is focused and exclusive at relevant theological points, but ambiguous and umbrella-like on broad sociopolitical matters — as though it were reaching to include participants on the verge of bowing out.

Both attempts represent a concrete convergence of thought within each distinct community. But while the climax of JPIC is specific direction on how churches and governments should act, Oxford's tendency is to talk mainly in theological language. The vagueness of the Oxford Declaration with regard to recognizing and affirming the distinct responsibilities of various cultural institutions makes it appear all dressed up with nowhere to go.

JPIC: A Manifesto for the New Age

JPIC is both movement and treatise, unveiled in March as part of a WCC "conciliar process" intended to clarify a new orthodoxy and to result in "common and binding pronouncements and actions on the urgent questions of the survival of mankind." The "Final Document" that emerged from Seoul was the third major draft and also the culmination of years of work aimed at redefining ecumenical faith and practice. While the outcome was less than the organizers may have hoped for, their goals were substantially achieved.

The early drafts of the JPIC document foresaw the emergence of an order that would integrate global environmental concerns into existing justice and peace movements in the churches — a union of liberation theology and a newer "green" theology. The working document called for specific "acts of covenanting" by the churches with "peoples' movements," liberation movements, peace groups, and the earth. These covenants would give "confessional status" to such specific actions as altering "the present international economic order and the debt crisis," "the demilitarization of international relations," and "the protection of the earth's atmosphere, the warming of the atmosphere, [fighting] the 'Greenhouse effect' and the energy problem." Further, taking these actions was equated with actualizing the kingdom of God. The second draft stated: "Affirming justice, peace and the integrity of creation as an integral part of our confession of faith in the Triune God is to proclaim the Realm of God."

However, the convocation in Seoul was unable to enact fully the comprehensive statement presented to it. Orthodox delegates objected to some critical theological terms, which were consequently set aside for the moment. The JPIC leadership has indicated that the theology guiding the development of the documents remains implicitly and will resurface for explicit address in future discussions. The main theological points of contention are as follows:

(1) JPIC statements posited an immanentist concept of God, which links the "Triune God" (Creator, Sustainer, Liberator) to creation and dilutes God's sovereignty over creation. Draft 2 proclaimed: "The primary work of the Triune God is to open the way towards fulfillment of the new creation *in our history* and the whole cosmos." JPIC hardly speaks of the personal, self-revealing Father, Son, and Holy Spirit who is Lord; rather, the voice of God is heard primarily in the "cries of the earth."

163

(2) JPIC's early drafts denied human uniqueness as the crown of creation in God's image. Humanity became "earth-keeper" first and foremost. God's image was described not as a quality of human nature but as a function: The human person is a creature with "certain gifts — reason, freedom, speech, manual dexterity — not to elevate it above the other wondrous creatures of God . . . but in order that it may image and reflect within the sphere of creation the tender care and compassion of the Creator."

JPIC theology denies the possibility of any positive view of human dominion as well. It is not corruption of the practice or understanding of the biblical "cultural mandate" that is sin, but the traditional doctrine of humankind itself that is at fault according to JPIC. In a reference to a 1967 article by historian Lynn White, which was a major influence in turning the churches' attention to ecological matters, the working draft stated that "it is said with some justification that our 'high' anthropology constitutes the major factor in the 'historic roots of our ecologic crisis.' "

(3) The early drafts made the earth "sacramental in character" and equated redemption with renewal of the earth while neglecting personal atonement. Fallenness is rooted in violations of the natural order and specific exploitative activity. The second person of the Trinity is translated into one who identifies with creation and challenges violations of it; he is not presented as one who reconciles humankind through his sacrificial death. There is no crucifixion and resurrection in JPIC theology.

Political and social changes — such as the events in Eastern Europe and new assessments of ecological disaster predictions — also challenged some of the specific political and economic analyses. Groups with specific concerns — the reunification of Korea, support for Palestinian statehood, condemnation of racism — forced these items on the agenda. And all the limits inherent in a multilingual drafting and amending process involving hundreds of delegates were displayed.

The result was a substantially watered down statement — but one that retained, in muted form, all of the theological and political orientations of the early drafts. The controversies did not make the theology more orthodox. Instead, the controversial issues were put aside for later adoption. The theology also allowed the drafters to undertake a radical critique of human economic activity. The document and all the subsequent activities it points to promise to dominate the agenda of the ecumenical world for years.

The final draft concludes with political covenants that mandate action in four areas: (1) creation of "a just economic order" and "liberation from bondage of the debt crisis," (2) demilitarization of international relations, (3) "preserving the earth's atmosphere," specifically from global warming and noxious emissions, and (4) the eradication of racism. Within these categories are specific commitments to action, such as: accepting limits to economic growth in favor of "sustainability" in resources, socially responsible investing by all churches, cancellation of international debt held by poor countries, abolition of nuclear weapons, banning of chlorofluorocarbons, an international tax on carbon dioxide emissions, and combating deforestation.

These policies are presented as covenant commitments within an overall new confession of faith and work for the 1990s and beyond. They are framed as *the* most critical concerns facing humanity and the church. The confession gives new status to the view that describes human cultivation and development as an intrusion into the sacred earth. It requires a comprehensive global reordering, a "realized eschatology" of profound, and perhaps revolutionary, consequences. This orientation ensures that thorough and balanced economic and political analysis will receive little account, and that worst case scenarios will rule the day.

The Oxford process bills itself as a discussion of economic principles from a Christian perspective, but its final document shows more unity on theology than on economics. The Declaration itself is essentially a discussion of relevant theological themes that form a starting point for reflection on the development of a just public order. One can only guess at the reasons the document is limited in its conclusions on economics. Some of the factors may be inadequate time, lack of consensus, and a more general failure of evangelicals to translate theology into specific economic, political, and policy-level discussion.

Fortunately, at the theological level, the Oxford Declaration comes closer to satisfying those looking for a way to tie together many strands of thought about the shape of Christian responsibility in the world. The Oxford Declaration is unabashedly orthodox and evangelical in its theological affirmations. The Bible is held as the supreme authority on faith and conduct, and God is acknowledged as sovereign in ruling over creation. The focus of the subsequent theology is the God-human-creation relationship: "Much of human aggression toward creation stems from a false understanding of the nature of creation and the human role in it." While humans were designed to exercise dominion over the earth, they do not have "licence to abuse" it. This implies the need to maintain a healthy ecological system over time. Failure in exercising this careful stewardship usually results from either a "selfish individualism" that neglects human community or a "rigid collectivism" that stifles human freedom.

This framework is explicitly designed to allow for the possibility of creative, productive cultivation of the earth with the use of technology. Specific directions are given, however, to set limits on this use of technology in order to protect the environment and prevent the disintegration of various forms of human community. The important thing is that humans be allowed to "express their creativity in service to others."

Work is inherently good, as defined by Oxford, not just a means to other ends. This goes for both the prospective worker and the prospective employer. Workers should not be reduced to "costs" or "labor inputs" and should be able to participate meaningfully in decision-making processes and should have opportunity for self-improvement through employment. Oxford goes so far as to suggest a "right" to work, along with a corresponding "obligation" of the community to provide employment opportunities — though how the "community" should do this is not clear.

A discussion of poverty follows from the discussion of work. God is said to be the "defender of the poor" when the poor are oppressed. This apparently is meant to suggest that not all poverty is completely due to external or structural causes and that some poverty may be primarily due to individual irresponsibility. "The causes of poverty are many and complex," asserts Oxford. The challenge for the future is to do two things: "analyse and explain the conditions to promote the creation of wealth" — a focus typically expressed by those in the conservative sociopolitical ethos — "as well as those that determine the distribution of wealth" — a focus typical of the liberal sociopolitical ethos. What seems to hold these formerly divergent views together in Oxford is the affirmation that injustice is not reducible simply to monetary or consumer deprivation. In the larger sense, poverty has its roots in "powerlessness." Thus, the theme of empowering the poor to take a place in community and responsibility for it implies "helping the poor to help themselves and be the subjects of their own development."

Fundamental to this sense of community is a polity built on *a priori* rights — to life and to freedom of religion, speech, and assembly.

While Oxford states that no political system is directly prescribed by Scripture, democracy receives qualified support because of the various elements associated almost exclusively with it — namely, limited government, a distinction between state and society, the rule of law, and a significant amount of nongovernment ownership of property, among others. Dispersed ownership of "the means of production" in a market or "mixed" economy is noted as "a significant component of democracy" that has the capacity to prevent totalitarianism. This preference for decentralized power is reinforced by the affirmation of "mediating structures" (family, church, etc.) that provide "other opportunities for loyalty." These are affirmed as vital, yet with little development of their specific roles in the creational order.

Despite this recognition of a plurality of institutions that make up the public order, Oxford is virtually devoid of any suggestions regarding the appropriate responsibility of each for the health of the public order. The Declaration also appears to use the pronoun "we" to indicate a sense of shared responsibility. But little is said about the means or institutions by which this responsibility is best fulfilled. For example, Oxford says that "individual self-interest can legitimately be pursued, but only in a context marked by the pursuit of the good of others." This is a balanced affirmation of the possibility of positive-sum political economy, but it says nothing about what qualifies or conditions the motive and practice of self-interest so that it legitimately enhances the "good of others." Do governments have a role in facilitating this? Do labor unions? Do political parties? Would they all do it in the same way? No answer can be found in Oxford. The above-quoted statement, lacking in an understanding of the givenness of various cultural institutions, can be taken in such different directions at the policy level as to negate the agreement between "liberals" and "conservatives" over it.

Despite these limitations in the Oxford Declaration, the attempt deserves great praise. Though the document has limited utility, its emergence demonstrates a needed exercise of leadership on these matters within a very decentralized evangelical community. Moreover, the interdisciplinary and inclusive (in geographical representation, as well as policy persuasions) character of the process stands as a model for other attempts by Christians to approach contemporary issues from the standpoint of an orthodox Christian worldview. The thoughtful work by the participants, many of whom surely have devoted much of their lives to the issues at hand, stands in contrast to the fads and fetishes that too often rule in many parts of the American evangelical world.

Comparing Oxford and JPIC

A dialogue between proponents of Oxford and JPIC would provide an enlightening amplification of the issues each raises. Some important points of distinction between these two documents highlight the critical issues that guide them. Such points of distinction also indicate the essential differences between ecclesial and theological "cultures" and public philosophies at odds within Christendom — particularly between one whose are circumstantial and fluid and one whose authoritative reference points are transcendent and permanent.

Since no such discussion has occurred, we offer the following contrasts to suggest the form it might take. These six areas might also form the basis for discussion of these two documents, and the movements they represent, in educational and group settings.

Revelation

While Oxford begins with submission to Scripture and Christian tradition, JPIC listens to the urgent "cries" of the earth that compel humans to act. To Oxford God remains fully personal — revealed as Father, Son, Spirit; JPIC speaks of the "Triune" Creator, Sustainer, and Liberator in order to emphasize God's ties to the creation. JPIC proponents would find Oxford too narrow in its sources, while Oxford would indicate JPIC is inclusive to the point of apostasy.

Anthropology and Human Activity

Oxford holds that humans are uniquely in God's image with special responsibility for the creation. JPIC, by contrast, sees human "dominion" over culture as exploitative, and indicates that humanity, instead, needs to see itself as equal to all other created things. Both hold humanity responsible for the condition of the earth, but they differ drastically in regard to the nature of those responsibilities and to whom we are accountable.

Sin and Evil

In JPIC, sin is found primarily in the structures developed by human culture that divide and oppress. These structures must simply be rejected in favor of a revolutionary new consciousness based on the interconnectedness of all things. Oxford recognizes the extensiveness of evil and its social expressions, but seeks to reform existing social life according to God-given norms. Institutions have a valid existence in Oxford, whereas in JPIC such human creations prevent a return to a pristine state. Oxford sees man's personal alienation from God as central to the fact of evil; JPIC sees alienation as an effect, rather than the cause of brokenness in creation.

Redemption

JPIC limits its scope to the restoration of the earth and to earthly "peace and justice." The atoning work of Jesus has no particular place in the framework, nor does personal salvation. Oxford begins by acknowledging the particular redemption found in Christ, which affects the condition of the creation, and human responsibility for the creation.

Poverty

JPIC sees poverty as the result of structural injustice. Therefore, it stresses overhauling the structures — such as the international financial regime that allegedly produced the debt crisis. Little is said of empowering the poor directly, and nothing of their own responsibilities. Poverty in Oxford is said to have complex causes that cannot be reduced to structures of oppression dominated by the rich. Oxford finds the roots of economic poverty in powerlessness. Since "work" — the cultivation of creation — is a profoundly good and human task, the poor need to be helped by the community so that they may help themselves and make a contribution to the community.

Policy

JPIC makes large leaps from theological premises to specific policy

169

prescriptions without any intervening steps to show their relationship. It simply assumes that the analysis presented requires radical measures. Oxford similarly makes a big jump from theology to a select list of pressing issues, but makes no attempt to design specific public policies. For JPIC, correct policy is intrinsic to faithfulness and confession. For Oxford, policy making is a part of a larger faithful response to the ongoing work of God in history, and it does not demand that consensus can or ought to be obtained on specific prescriptions.

Both of these documents are major milestones in ongoing dialogue and study within the communities in which they appear. They represent for Christians two distinct approaches to modern problems and distinct agendas for the next decade. The greatest significance of their appearance is thay they indicate the new circumstances of interdependence, economic sensitivity, environmental effects of highly organized human actions, and the changing nature of international political activity facing the church and its mission. These undertakings deserve analysis and continual attention as the church assesses its call to faithfulness within the moment in history that God has placed it.

Yet both documents exemplify the limitations of consensus declarations. They aim at demonstrating unity and downplay the discussion of legitimate differences that might actually enrich the ends they seek. And they tend to be general: Oxford names no specific research tasks to undertake, and neither document poses questions for future consideration.

JPIC extends these weaknesses beyond the convocation that affirmed it. By demanding unity and interconnectedness, the document requires not discussion and dialogue, but conformity and acceptance. It takes the stance of authoritative confession; no further questions are to be asked. It requires acceptance of scientific, political, and economic conclusions that are still subject to debate. And it seeks to require the churches of the world to concentrate resources and education on major efforts in environmental activism.

What might have been useful in JPIC's sense of urgency about the need to tackle certain current issues is wasted in its hysterical apocalyptic prophecy and ideological hectoring. Oxford, in contrast, offers the most promise for faithful action. It opens the possibility of dialogue, even as it falls short of identifying the next step for its work. The signers and participants in the Oxford Conference need to lay out public tasks, economic and political research to be undertaken, issues to be resolved. They must be not so much satisfied with their delight in finding common ground as motivated to move and work in ways that will continue to develop insight for Christians working in various arenas and institutions — including the church, which is responsible to nurture Christian reflection for wise public action and scholarship.

PART IV

A Good Beginning, but Much More Needs to be Done

James W. Skillen

The Oxford Declaration should provoke Christians to some creative thinking about the meaning of economic justice at the end of the twentieth century. A new way may now be opening for critical consideration of economic matters from a Christian perspective — a viewpoint that will amount to more than simply an accommodation to liberalism or Marxism. Communist experiments have collapsed in large part because of economic failure. Free market liberalism has been around much longer and has had more opportunities to prove itself. But still, in the West and elsewhere in the world, many economic as well as social problems remain unresolved under capitalist systems — problems of environmental depletion, employment of the poor and ill-trained, and international movements of technology, money, and labor.

Many of the signers of the Oxford Declaration have been doing serious writing and research, so the document is an outgrowth of more than merely a few days of conversation. Think, for example, of conference organizer Ronald J. Sider's *Rich Christians in an Age of Hunger,*[1] of Bob Goudzwaard's *Capitalism and Progress,*[2] of Ronald H. Nash's *Poverty and Wealth: The Christian Debate Over Capitalism,*[3] and of Richard C. Chewning's four-volume series on biblical principles and economics, *Christians in the Market Place.*[4]

1. Downers Grove: InterVarsity, 1984.
2. Grand Rapids: Eerdmans, 1979.
3. Westchester: Crossway, 1986.
4. Colorado Springs: Navpress, 1989-90.

The Declaration begins with a Christ-centered confession of faith that affirms, among other things, that the Scriptures are "our supreme authority in all matters of faith and conduct," and that God "made a perfect world for human beings created to live in fellowship with God." Moreover, as a matter of first importance, the document affirms the biblical testimony that "justice is basic to Christian perspectives on economic life." "Justice expresses God's actions to restore God's provision to those who have been deprived and to punish those who have violated God's standards."

Creation and Stewardship

The first major section of the Declaration starts with creation. Several basic biblical principles are summarized — all quite well. God is the creator and *owner* of all things. Human beings are called to be "stewards" of what God owns. "The greatness of creation — both human and non-human — exists to glorify its Creator."

Sin is the root of greed, ecological destruction, neglect of the poor, and other economic evils. The foundations of a healthy economy are to be found in the right order of creation's relation to God — and, consequently, in the right relations among all creatures. Sin is the distortion of these right relations because of disobedience to God.

> The dominion which God gave human beings over creation (Genesis 1:30) does not give them licence to abuse creation. First, they are responsible to God, in whose image they were made, not to ravish creation but to sustain it, as God sustains it in divine providential care. Second, since human beings are created in the image of God for community and not simply as isolated individuals (Genesis 1:28), they are to exercise dominion in a way that is responsible to the needs of the total human family, including future generations. (6)

Up to this point, the Declaration is an inspirational confession, highlighting some fundamental biblical teachings. But beginning with paragraph 8, the document jumps quickly to contemporary society without having laid a sufficient basis for explaining the development of economic institutions in God's creation — an institutional development that has led in our day to the formation of major corporations, massive accumulations of capital, extensive migrations of people for employment, and a highly complex diversity of economic, educational, familial, and political organizations unlike anything known in biblical times.

Why should this be a problem for a declaration such as this? After all, a brief declaration can hardly be expected to do what a textbook or theological treatise can do. The difficulty, as we will try to show, is that the statement allows important differences in economic judgment among the signers to be covered over by general confessional statements. Instead of sharpening the meaning of *economic* agreement among Christians, the statement allows one set of words to serve an equivocal purpose — to be interpreted in different ways by those who differ over economic policies and principles.

If the purpose of the statement were simply to show that those who hold different economic views can nonetheless agree on a basic Christian confession about life, then it serves a wonderful purpose. But if the statement is intended to point the way toward a potentially new *economic* agreement from a Christian perspective, then its greatest weaknesses appear precisely at those points where it needs to be the strongest. We will try to illustrate this in what follows.

In referring to the legitimacy of productivity in God's creation (paragraph 8), for example, the statement says, "In assessing economic systems from a Christian perspective, we must consider their ability both to generate and to distribute wealth and income justly." This is a good and true statement, but it takes for granted the phrase "economic systems," and the very meaning of those words is a big question today. For some, an "economic system" is a highly political entity; for others it is something that ought to be largely independent of the political sphere. Moreover, Christians might be able to agree that the generation and distribution of wealth and income should be just, but they are also likely to disagree over the meaning of both "justice" and "generation and distribution."

Paragraphs 9 and 10 continue this problematic momentum. The words "technology," "industrialization," and "corporations" (to mention but three) are used in paragraphs that essentially serve to affirm the agreement of the signers that "we must search for ways to use appropriate technology responsibly according to every cultural context." But the meaning of "we" becomes increasingly ambiguous because the kinds of responsibility to which the Declaration wants to call

177

Christians in different "cultural contexts" are necessarily spread out differently among governments, corporations, households, individuals, and so forth. All the signers agree, for example, that "technology should not foster disintegration of family or community, or function as an instrument of social domination." But who is responsible in what institutional ways to make sure that such disintegration does not take place? The Declaration does not say.

Consider but one illustration. A variety of different modern technologies have led to the disintegration of rural communities in the United States and throughout the world. The world is becoming increasingly urbanized. Over the past four generations of American families, a majority of the population has moved from farms and small towns into major urban areas. Less than 4 percent of the population now lives on farms. Depending on one's outlook, especially if one treasures the values of family coherence, hard work, and a simple lifestyle, this development might be viewed as highly unhealthy. Or it might be viewed as a major step forward in making possible a development of talents and institutional creativity that rural people would never have had the opportunity to experience. Free market advocates might be more optimistic about the good achieved by this movement; those with a more communal orientation might be more pessimistic. The point of my criticism is simply that the generally positive theological statement in paragraphs 8-12 on the use of technology does not take us very far into an understanding of the criteria for judging responsible technology.

Paragraph 11 perhaps best illustrates the critical point in this section.

> We urge individuals, private institutions, and governments everywhere to consider both the local, immediate, and the global, long term ecological consequences of their actions. We encourage corporate action to make products which are more "environmentally friendly." And we call on governments to create and enforce just frameworks of incentives and penalties which will encourage both individuals and corporations to adopt ecologically sound practices.

While this paragraph recognizes a diversity of institutions by listing them, it in no way tries to suggest what their different responsibilities are. It is an appeal to people in general to produce better outcomes. But the desired ecologically sound outcomes will depend on quite different

178

responsibilities of each. Thus, to say that governments should create and enforce just frameworks and incentives can be interpreted in radically different ways with respect to concrete policy proposals. The Declaration does not articulate standards by which to judge the actions of governments as it seeks to create and enforce sound practices. We would hope that all Christians can agree to this statement, but it does not go very far in indicating what the institutional and policy consequences should be.

Work and Leisure

The second major section of the document considers work and leisure. Again, some basic biblical material is introduced and summarized in a worthy fashion. Work "is central to the Creator's intention for humanity" and has "intrinsic value." "Christians should do their work in the service of God and humanity." "The deepest meaning of human work is that the almighty God established human work as a means to accomplish God's work in the world." "Human work has consequences that go beyond the preservation of creation to the anticipation of the eschatological transformation of the world." Sin distorts the meaning of work both with respect to the service of God and with respect to the service of fellow human beings. Sin is what leads to alienation and pain in our labor. "People should never be treated in their work as mere means." And yet they are. Work is service, and yet in sin it becomes highly self-interested. Women and "marginalised groups" are especially discriminated against in work.

While this section does not say much about the redemptive restoration of work through Jesus Christ, it does affirm that God's redemptive purpose is to overcome the evils brought on by sin. Therefore, the God of the Bible "condemns exploitation and oppression." People everywhere should be restored to meaningful work. "It is a freedom right, since work in its widest sense is a form of self-expression."

Yet here again, the broad statements that should win agreement from many different Christians can be interpreted in different ways, and the differences are not articulated. Consider, for example, paragraph 26:

The right to earn a living would be a positive or sustenance right. Such a right implies the obligation of the community to provide

179

employment opportunities. Employment cannot be guaranteed where rights conflict and resources may be inadequate. However the fact that such a right cannot be enforced does not detract in any way from the obligation to seek the highest level of employment which is consistent with justice and the availability of resources.

What does this paragraph really say? It implies that people have a right. But a right to be claimed against whom, by appeal to what authority? Who has the authority to decide whether or not sufficient resources are available to make employment possible for those who claim the right to work? And who is obligated to seek the highest level of employment consistent with justice and the availability of resources? What is "the community" referred to here? At what point is a high level of employment inconsistent with justice, and why? Obviously, behind the Declaration's statement are dozens of unstated assumptions and points of disagreement on economic policies and institutional responsibilities. Free market advocates will say that a high level of employment made possible by high levels of taxation and redistribution is unjust. More liberal economists will say that the "community" may justly redistribute some resources in order to help make work available for those who have a right to work. This paragraph takes for granted a highly differentiated society in which governments, corporations, and many institutions hold different degrees of responsibility for work, but it does not help to illumine the character and obligations of that complex society.

The few brief paragraphs on leisure and rest properly emphasize the need for enjoyment and relaxation, for worship on the sabbath, and for avoidance of workaholism. What is disappointing, however, is that these paragraphs do not emphasize the vision of eschatological *fulfillment* of work itself in God's kingdom. The sabbath rest, after all, is not just a good habit for our lives in this age: It is anticipatory of the final sabbath feast, of the day when the great Master says "well done, good and faithful servant." The Declaration says that rest "consists in the enjoyment of nature as God's creation, in the free exercise and development of abilities which God has given to each person, in the cultivation of fellowship with one another, and above all, in delight in communion with God." While this is true about rest, these sentences should also be used to describe the meaning of work in this world. Rest and leisure should not be connected with real human enjoyment while work is left in the realm of drudgery and lack of communion with God. The biblical meaning of *rest* shines through when we see that it points as a sign to the ultimate fulfillment of our *labors,* our *work,* in the kingdom of God.

Poverty and Justice

The third major section of the Declaration deals with the primary "problem" that economists are always trying to solve: poverty. God did not intend that there should be any poverty, according to the statement. Moreover, God is the "defender of the poor" (Ps. 146:7-9). We are called to help the poor and to help overcome poverty.

What are the causes of poverty? They are "many and complex" — ranging from "cultural attitudes and actions taken by social, economic, political and religious institutions" to natural disasters.

Whatever the causes of poverty — and all causes should be studied — the Bible's call for justice demands that special attention be given to the poor. The "common link" in the Bible between widows, orphans, resident aliens, wage earners, slaves, and the poor "is powerlessness by virtue of economic and social needs. The justice called forth is to restore these groups to the provision God intends for them." Individuals, families, churches, and governments are all responsible to aid the poor. And justice

> may also require socio-political actions that enable the poor to help themselves and be the subjects of their own development and the development of their communities. We believe that we and the institutions in which we participate are responsible to create an environment of law, economic activity, and spiritual nurture which creates these conditions.

Here again, the statement affirms an undoubted good, namely, that people should help the poor and that the poor should help themselves. Everyone is responsible somehow. But these paragraphs in themselves do not convince me that we should or should not ask our federal government to spend more money on a jobs program for the unemployed. They do not let me see why it would or would not be good to increase state aid to the hungry through food stamp supplements. Both those who believe in greater government involvement and those who believe in fewer government initiatives can affirm what is said in this declaration without indicating what they mean by these words.

This section concludes with paragraphs on the world debt crisis, inflation, military expenditures, the drug crisis, and several other matters that greatly affect the poor. But the admonitions do not lead very far. For example, "both lenders and borrowers shared in creating this [global] debt. The result has been increasing impoverishment of the people. Both lenders and borrowers must share responsibility for finding solutions." Or, regarding the two "key agents" responsible for the drug trade, the "rich markets which consume drugs must end their demand. And the poorer countries which produce them must switch to other products." This is not very powerful or insightful.

While I am criticizing these somewhat superficial appeals for good to be done, I should point out that the conferees who signed this declaration also spent considerable time developing a separate document that is more detailed in its attention to "credit-based income generation programs." I will not comment on that document here, but perhaps in its greater detail, the reader will find ideas, principles, and a framework of argument that is illustrative of how one might deal with these other issues that the group touched on so lightly.

Freedom, Government, and Economics

The loaded burden of the Oxford Declaration really becomes evident in this fourth and concluding section. Although the ambiguous language of "rights" has been used earlier in the document, here, beginning in paragraph 49, the writers finally acknowledge that the language of rights is not always clear. "Therefore," they say, "it is important to have clear criteria for what defines rights." The next four paragraphs attempt to clarify the Christian meaning of rights.

> In seeking human rights we search for an authority or norm which transcends our situation. God is that authority; God's character constitutes that norm. Since human rights are a priori rights, they are not conferred by the society or the state. Rather, human rights are rooted in the fact that every human being is made in the image of God. The deepest ground of human dignity is that while we were yet sinners, Christ died for us (Romans 5:8). (50)

This is not an entirely clear statement, however. Several unanswered questions remain: What is the relation between God's authority and that of the state and society? If human rights are grounded in God's creation of us in the divine image, then do we have no one other than God to whom to appeal for the recognition of those rights? In what respect does human dignity require recognition by various God-appointed human authorities? And what is the relation between Christ's death for us and our original created character as the image of God?

The next paragraph (51) goes on to affirm that God's justice for human beings "requires life, freedom, and sustenance." But it does not go beyond reference to God's justice to clarify which human institutions should do what to affirm or protect human rights, though it does take for granted such human responsibility: "It is a requirement of justice that human beings, including refugees and stateless persons, are able to live in society with dignity. Human beings therefore have a claim on other human beings for social arrangements that ensure that they have access to the sustenance that makes life in society possible." But how do human beings make claims on one another? An answer to this question would require the articulation of different institutional identities and responsibilities such as the claims of children on their parents, of students on their teachers, of citizens on governments, and so forth.

Leaving this matter of human rights up in the air, the Declaration moves on to a consideration of democracy, declaring that "no political system is directly prescribed by Scripture," but "Biblical values and historical experience call Christians to work for the adequate participation of all people in the decision-making processes on questions that affect their lives." This modest vote for democracy is also problematic. Consider this question, for example: What kind of participation is "adequate" in what kinds of institutions, since *all* "decision-making processes" affect people's lives? The signers are surely not calling for the radical democratization of families, are they? What about business enterprises? Even with respect to political life, who is to decide what is adequate democratic representation? Why should we even view democracy as somehow being in accord with God's authority and character?

In this section the document makes repeated reference to what "historical experience" teaches.

Recent history suggests that a dispersion of ownership of the means of production is a significant component of democracy. Monopolistic

ownership, either by the state, large economic institutions, or oligarchies is dangerous. Widespread ownership, either in a market
economy or a mixed system, tends to decentralise power and prevent
totalitarianism. (56)

These statements sound like the contribution of the more conservative
authors of the document. Clearly, "recent history" must be the collapse
of communist governments in Eastern Europe. Communism does not
work, and capitalism does. But what kind of democratic capitalism
should satisfy Christians? What parts of history are instructive to us and
why? These paragraphs do not answer these questions. They say less
about what targets ought to be hit, and more about what ought to be
avoided, namely, totalitarianism. But how widely dispersed should
ownership be? And how vigorous should government be in forcing
decentralization?

The next paragraphs (57-59) continue this theme, lauding the
general economic merits of market-oriented economies over centrally
planned economies. And the Declaration then acknowledges that the
relation of the economy to other institutions becomes all the more urgent
a concern in a free market society.

As non-capitalist countries increasingly turn away from central planning and towards the market, the question of capitalism's effect on
culture assumes more and more importance. The market system can
be an effective means of economic growth, but can, in the process,
cause people to think that ultimate meaning is found in the accumulation of more goods. There is also the danger that the model of the
market, which may work well in economic transactions, will be
assumed to be relevant to other areas of life, and people may consequently believe that what the market encourages is therefore best
or most true. (59)

All of this is to say that a free market economy does not answer all of
life's questions. But the Oxford document does not really tell us much
about the way in which a free market economy helps people realize the
meaning of work, stewardship, leisure, technology, and justice in the
service of God and neighbors.

In paragraphs 60-62, the document returns to the role of government, but stays at a level of generality that covers over disagreements.

184

It says, among other things, that "significant decisions about local human communities are usually best made at a level of government most directly responsible to the people affected." "At a minimum, government must establish a rule of law that protects life, secures freedom, and provides basic security. Special care must be taken to make sure the protection of fundamental rights is extended to all members of society, especially the poor and oppressed (Proverbs 31:8-9; Daniel 4:27)." But why stress the "minimum" task of government — and not declare what its high calling before God ought to be, from a Christian point of view? And who is supposed to take "special care" that "fundamental rights" are extended to all members of society? Is government supposed to do this? If so, what are the fundamental rights it is supposed to uphold in contrast to the human rights that parents, employers, or church authorities are supposed to uphold or enforce?

> The provision of sustenance rights is also an appropriate function of government. Such rights must be carefully defined so that government's involvement will not encourage irresponsible behaviour and the breakdown of families and communities. In a healthy society, this fulfilment of rights will be provided through a diversity of institutions so that the government's role will be that of last resort. (62)

This is an example of where the document's approach to concreteness leads to confusion. If it is appropriate for the government to provide sustenance rights, then why should it do so only as a last resort? Why is that normative? Which institutions are responsible as the first, second, and third resort? If parents should sustain their children and employers should sustain their employees, then may children and employees ever appeal to the government to enforce their right to sustenance from their parents and employers? Or should individuals be able to go to the government directly if they are hungry, without housing, or in need of further education? The Declaration does not help us answer these questions.

Paragraph 63 introduces the concept of "mediating structures" but does so in a way that makes no direct connection between such structures and the economy. The purpose of these structures seems to be primarily to serve as a means of decreasing the need for centralized government and a way of influencing other institutions. But what are they in themselves, and where do they fit into a document on economics?

185

I wish that the Oxford Declaration had stated boldly that the signers were aware that they had drafted a document that covered over their differences as well as affirmed their confessional agreement as Christians. It would have been more useful, perhaps, had it outlined the tasks yet to be done for Christians to work out a more complete *economic* perspective for the complex and detailed realities of contemporary society.

This is not to say that the Declaration is not useful and encouraging. That it manifests the fruits of Christian community is an encouragement in itself. We thank all those who labored on it as a means of bringing Christians together who might otherwise have stayed apart. But a casual reader could come away from this document believing that it really is a statement of principles, when in fact, it is a general Christian confession about life with some reference to a variety of economically connected realities. It does not go very far in articulating a Christian understanding of economics, production, business, labor, public policy, and the responsibilities of the multiple institutions of our society for economic justice. That remains to be done. We can hope, therefore, that this document will encourage Christians who hold different economic views to keep on working together.